Join an epic journey of discovery, adventure and changing young lives...

Book coaching: The Business Ghost
Copy editing: Theresa Finley
Cover design, typesetting and publishing: Plum Design & Publishing Ltd

ISBN: 978-1-7390969-0-8

Published in United Kingdom in September 2022 by Kudos Publishing.

www.brashsolutions.co.uk

To learn more about the Pepper Foundation, please visit:
www.pepper.org.uk

DEDICATION

To Jamie and Boo,
I hope you get a little inspiration to always seek out new and exciting adventures, to keep your party balloons of life fully inflated.

And to my wife Penny for your love and support (and patience).

Thank you everyone who supported me or took part in this adventure - see you for the next one!

A special thanks to:

Tony Denton, Richard Hillier, David Roberts, Simon Cole, Michael Fairrie, Tim Mayes, Keith Tucker, Tony Brash, Stephen Pike at The Marble and Granite Centre, Sarah and Nick Roach at Just Go.

In loving memory of my father,
Bob Brash (1944 - 2013)
and our dear friend,
Anne Consedine (1972 - 2019)

FOREWORD

By Pat Daley

Chair of The Pepper Foundation

As the Chair of The Pepper Foundation, I was honoured when Richard asked me to write the foreword to his inspiring book, with all its tales of adventure and life lessons filling every page. Richard approached Pepper in 2014 with his plan to undertake a 28-day challenge around Britain using only pedal power, foot power, swim power and rowing power. We thought the whole idea sounded a little ambitious, but we had grown familiar with Richard's escapades over the years, so we were right behind him, and the best part was that he would donate the money raised to support Pepper's work.

Firstly, a brief history of The Pepper Foundation. We are a small charity raising money to help fund Children's Hospice at Home nursing care in Bucks and Herts. The funds we raise support specialist nurses who provide paediatric care (free of charge in patients' own homes) for children with life-limiting or life-threatening conditions. The nurses work for the Children's Hospice at Home nursing team, which manages the service they provide. We started from small beginnings in 1990 when Robert Breakwell, a local man, decided to fundraise for cancer care by putting on a charity concert after The Children's Hospice nurses had nursed his wife through the final months of her life. Named after the famous Beatles album, Sgt Pepper's Lonely Hearts Club Band, the show was called The Pepper Show. And every year since then, except where national pandemics deemed it undoable, the Pepper Show (which can be loosely called a rock concert) with local musicians, singers and production team has run six concerts of joyous music with high-performance values, generating much-needed funds.

The show led to the birth of the Foundation, and it has been growing ever since, with people like Richard contributing their efforts and many other volunteers and tireless workers getting involved.

Back to Bonkers Brash – we were excited and enthusiastic about supporting Richard to get this show on the road (rivers, sea and off the beaten track), but whilst we are experienced fundraisers, we had never done anything like this before. We were keen to promote the challenge wherever we could and knew that, while Richard was busy planning the details of his journey, we should be shouting about it and sourcing financial support. We worked with Richard to find corporate sponsors who could supply the vehicle to transport him and all his gear and provide a bed when needed. We also helped source sponsorship for food and supplies to keep him safe and sustained while travelling. We found a volunteer driver, Tony Denton, to provide logistics support to Richard throughout the journey, and several members of our team were there to cheer him along the way.

Promotion of the challenge was crucial, and we managed to arrange various local TV and radio shout outs along with some local newspaper coverage. As you will learn in the pages of the book, there are always lessons to learn and things you look back on to see where more could have been done. So the next time Richard ventures out on a bonkers challenge, be ready, dear reader, as we might just get in touch.

Everyone at Pepper and all our sponsors excitedly and occasionally anxiously followed Richard's progress day-by-day on the Bonkers Brash social media channels, and a team of us were there to meet on Bournemouth beach at the finish. It was a very emotional moment to see him arrive home safely and on time, and it is only by reading this book that any of us can even start to appreciate what it was like for him during that month on the road. We were immensely proud of Richard's achievement on Bournemouth beach, celebrating alongside Richard's family and friends with our yellow balloons and welcome home banners.

Bonkers Brash raised £17k for The Pepper Foundation, and we are delighted he has asked for the profits from this book to grow that total even further.

INTRODUCTION

According to Etymology Online, the word 'bonkers' originated in the 1940s as naval slang for someone a little bit drunk. It later evolved into a general, lighthearted term for outrageous behaviour or pushing the boundaries of social norms. I have adopted it because it sounds so alliteratively pleasing alongside my surname, and I have spent my whole life trying to find where those boundaries are hiding.

The older you get, the more it dawns on you just how little time we have on this planet. And how quickly the number that society tells us we must use to display our passage through life adds up! The title of this book is not a reference to any specific person's terminal diagnosis or even to highlight the life-limiting circumstances some have to deal with from birth. The twenty-eight is a reference to a story, but the number could be any number, just like the days or years we each get to live are as ambiguous, random and uncontrollable as any other roll of the dice.

I wrote this book because I am old enough to remember a time when all my friends and I did after school and at weekends was go and play outside. We were carefree (probably a little too careless at times), adventurous, fearless, ambitious and always looking for more of that mysterious substance we knew as fun. Having children of my own in an age where adventure is viewed through a screen rather than experienced in person and communication is virtual far more than face-to-face, I can see the difference. I work in technology and love the latest gadgets and advancements in digital communications and superfast everything: I completely understand that we need to push those boundaries and improve ourselves. But I think we are smart enough, as a race, to make the best of both worlds and see two sides of the horizon. I believe we should recognise that the most limited, valuable resource we have is time and embrace it with both hands. Living our own life to the full and making the world a better place. To do that, you have to learn to appreciate – and that is what this book is about.

I sincerely hope you enjoy the adventure, and I would be overjoyed if it inspired you to help causes like the one The Pepper Foundation is devoted to supporting. But I also want you to be inspired personally. So, as you read, keep in mind these three things:

1. Life is short, and nobody on their last day on earth ever said, 'I wish I had spent more time in the office'. If you did have twenty-eight days to live (and this is a value exercise, not a scary one, so let's remove the fear or sadness), what would you do with that precious time?
2. We live in a world of rules and restraints, but how many of them are laws? Is there a law against you going on an adventure or breaking free of what society tells you is modern life? Will your heart really stop beating if separated from your phone for more than an hour? Does a documentary about nature in far off countries you will never visit even come close to the wildlife within a mile of your house? And when did you stop and think about the opportunities you have yet to live, especially in comparison to so many who are less fortunate than you?
3. Unless you are reading this book from a prison cell, you are not a prisoner. You have a choice about how you live your life. You don't need to drink to be bonkers, and who cares if you stand out for pushing the boundaries. Maybe your love of life and sense of adventure might inspire someone else, and together we can introduce a bit more bonkers into the world.

CONTENTS

CHAPTER ONE

YOU ARE DOING WHAT?

The sun was still rising above the water, glistening across the eastern horizon as I paddled out past the long concrete causeway. Surrounded by the ancient priory ruins, Tynemouth Castle stood behind me, and gentle sun-blessed waves jostled all around. I imagine my sea-facing view that morning was the same one the Benedictine monks who lived there 700 years before would have seen. Pure, unadulterated, unchanged for millennia, unblemished by human hands. Blue sea touching a golden sky. It was ancient, idyllic and beautiful.

As I rounded the small lighthouse at the end of the long sea barrier and crossed the mouth of the River Tyne, modern versions of another age-old practice were evident. I was delighted to meet a small group of fellow kayakers bobbing and smiling as they cast their lines into the perfect blueness. Whereas I was a journeyman traveller just passing by, these guys were professionals, up early and already working. They were fishermen out catching herring, and it was fun to talk to them about their work (what a life!) and tell them all about my adventure. After sharing stories, I left my new Geordie fisherman friends behind with mutual good wishes and a feeling of kinship that I still recall every time I have kippers for breakfast.

As I paddled south, past the river opening and down toward the landing site, I considered once more the why, what, and how of arriving at that tranquil place. The previous day, I had traversed the Scotland-England border across a quirky chain bridge, almost topped 50km per hour on a flat road on my bike (wow!), and joined a seal colony on their morning swim.

The following day, I rested: spending time reflecting on the challenges and triumphs behind and before me.

What is the value of why?

I am writing this book almost six years after starting a 28-day challenge to circumnavigate the UK using nothing but self-propulsion, self-belief and speedos. That meant doing a quadrathlon each day: running, swimming, cycling and kayaking. As I pen this particular chapter, it is March 2021, and the UK has spent most of the last 12 months in what we came to know as 'lockdown' caused by the COVID-19 pandemic. It is probably no exaggeration to say that my adventure, which we called the 'Bonkers Brash' challenge, was the complete opposite of being told not to leave your house unless it is absolutely vital. For that month, in July 2015, I had never felt freer.

This book is about freedom. It is about recognising that life can be limiting, so we owe it to ourselves to take hold of opportunities and live ours to the full, with both hands, and not let go. It has sub-themes of family, friends, perseverance, planning, appreciation, love, risk management, nature, pushing boundaries and giving generously – but it is essentially about appreciating freedom.

As word of the Bonkers Brash Around Britain Challenge started to spread throughout my contact base and beyond, it would always become a conversation topic. I enjoyed the reactions from quizzical looks, startled stares, momentary silences, concerned sideways glances to my longsuffering wife, Penny, and every display of emotion you could imagine. Some shared an awed, deep-thinking gaze that suggested the person was trying to imagine for themselves the size of the challenge and the drive behind it. Others became hyper-excited, visibly moved and asking ten questions a minute. What can I do to help? Can I join you? Are you supporting a charity? Where does your passion come from? (Actually, no one asked the 'passion' question, but I could imagine it being top of a Reality TV reporter's list.)

You could sum up all these questions in one word...why? The other way of asking 'why' has an entirely different meaning. It is the slightly sarcastic, certainly cynical and potentially patronising version which, by its very nature, can be frustrating when trying to set hugely ambitious goals. That 'why' often comes from the fear of the unknown and ignorance of what it means to push yourself beyond what you think you can be capable of. Living outside of your comfort zone and in effect being truly alive, as a full life requires two things: freedom and a desire for discovery. In my opinion, not wanting to understand why is to waste the privilege of being alive. It is failing to appreciate the simple gift of breathing in and out each day and missing the chance to explore the even greater wonders of experience. Where will your questioning take you?

Don't get me wrong; sometimes, life will present you with a crazy notion that has no value at all or an idea that it would be disastrous to pursue. Not every scheme is a smart one, and good intention does not steer everybody's drive or ambition. Some suggestions should be nipped in the bud before they get anywhere near a drawing board. But we should, at least, start by questioning every idea with an open mind.

I think it was Voltaire who said, *"Judge a man by his questions rather than his answers"*. Throughout history, humanity's most outstanding and astonishing achievements have come from someone pondering 'why', 'what if', or 'how'. Then that person, their friends and colleagues or others inspired by those thoughts set about answering the question for themselves. Questions that challenge limitations are usually the ones that open up the boundaries of potential.

People said I was crazy, reckless, out of my mind and that, by attempting this challenge, I would be putting my business at risk and neglecting my family. They really did! I was happy to admit to myself that the whole thing was a bit bonkers. But those who gave me the chance to explain, those that asked the right 'why' and listened, were ultimately able to engage with it themselves. Some brave adventurers did indeed join me for sections of the journey. My family and friends would appear from time to time to cheer me on the way, and a great many others helped by donating to The Pepper Foundation or simply by sending messages of encouragement and support.

Growth comes when you challenge the status quo

Imagine if no one had ever decided to try something new. Where would we be today? Think of all the great pioneers and adventurers who challenged frontiers, discovered new lands and uncovered ancient treasures. And the scientists, thinkers, and nonconformists who said, 'there must be a better way to…'. History is full of people who questioned the ordinary and achieved greatness for themselves, those around them, and generations to follow. When Sir Isaac Newton said, *"If I have seen further, it is by standing on the shoulders of giants"*, he inferred that what you do today can be a platform for someone else to do something similar or even more wonderful later.

I'm not suggesting that my Bonkers Brash Challenge compares with any of those incredible feats or the world-changing heroes who made them happen. I'm simply hoping that I can inspire you to push yourself a little further, dig a little deeper and see if there is more you can achieve today than you believed possible. And that's why I am writing this book six years after the event: because the last couple of years has taught me another important lesson. Time is precious, and life is for living and challenging your boundaries.

As you will know from the foreword, I wanted to raise some funds for a local charity as part of the challenge. I knew that not only would it give me more drive to succeed, it would also encourage support from others as there was no way it would be possible all on my own.

When it comes to charities, there is only ever one choice for any Bonkers Brash activity. Ever since completing the Three Peaks Challenge in 2000, when I first came across The Pepper Foundation, they have established a hold over a little corner of my heart. The fantastic people who work there and the life-enhancing support they give children with life-limiting conditions is all you need to know to fall in love with this incredible charity. And the more you know, the more you just want to help.

My compulsion for competing in endurance events has always been the adventure and hunger (which is still unfulfilled) to understand my personal limits. But alongside the accounts of my journey and stories of some extraordinary children whose treatments The Pepper Foundation helps fund, the thoughts in this book are really reflections on what I learned – then and every day since.

Back to that sun-soaked day on the Tyne

The morning I paddled and chatted with those fishermen at the mouth of the River Tyne was day twenty-one of the twenty-eight-day journey. It marked my return to England after spending ten days battling the dramatic and resplendent beauty of Scotland's coastline and weather. I've started my tale here because of the contrast it represented. It felt like the trek was in three parts: England going north, east across Scotland and finally back into England travelling south. Each of those stages delivered its own unique, overriding character, emotions and themes. This was by no means my first adventure, I have been doing crazy things and searching for my limits for as long as I can remember, but it was certainly the longest and most involved. I know you grow every time you do something like this, but I'm not sure I was aware of that progression until completing this challenge. It felt like I had grown a little wiser, more resilient and with a greater degree of preparedness and versatility on each stage of the journey.

The first part was like childhood. You are eager, full of energy, prone to rash decisions and easily swayed by circumstances beyond your control. You learn a lot in that stage of life – but usually only on reflection. The middle stage was hard; I can think of no other word for it. Traversing Scotland, for me, was like mid-life. Several crises were averted, and tiredness well and truly set in (I even fell asleep at the handle-bars once). But I managed to survive and pull on all I had learned previously to get me through. The final section was where I started to reflect and think about the whole expedition and what it meant to me personally. It appears as a downward slope on a map as the eastern coast of this grand island ripples along before swerving to the right and back again around East Anglia. Approaching fifty, I do feel a little like that is where I am at in life now. 'It is all downhill from here' is a curious phrase, and I often wonder: does that mean you're past your best days (the high points) or that it gets easier? I refuse to accept the best days are past, but I believe life gets easier (despite my body arguing the point) if you are prepared to live and learn diligently.

I know I have many adventure-filled days ahead and a long way to go before I hang up my peddles, paddles and running shoes, but I know I need to be more considered in the things I choose to do. Maybe that is why the morning with the fishermen, on my first day back in England, was so special to me. Or perhaps it just felt like the right place to start sharing my story. But here we are, and I hope you enjoy the rest of my tale and feel inspired to go off and seek some adventures of your own, whatever stage of your life you find yourself traversing.

DAY 1

My family in Bournemouth

Sponsors and Mayor at Just Go HQ in Bedfordshire

River Exe Swim

CHAPTER TWO

PREPARING FOR A MONTH OF MEMORIES

On Saturday the 4th of July 2015, Chile beat Argentina 4-1 on penalties, after an uneventful 0-0 draw to win the Copa América Cup Final for the first time in their history. That same day, in Brooklyn's Coney Island Hotdog-Eating Championship, Matt 'Megatoad' Stonie defeated eight-time winner Joey 'Jaws' Chestnut to cause the biggest upset in the competition's recent history, consuming 62 hot dogs in one sitting. And across the rest of America, most people were celebrating Independence Day. I wonder if you remember what you were doing that day?

I decided long ago that too many days could drift by unnoticed and unaccounted for if we're not mindful of the fact. Yes, there is the necessity of work and the labour of love involved in bringing up a family. I know I am privileged to have a job I enjoy and the freedom to work there on my terms. My wife and children are the most precious people in the world to me, and I hope I never take them for granted. But even with an appreciative mindset, the days and weeks can still come and go without leaving a trace in the mind. So, I made myself a promise to make more days count, find more experiences to enjoy and make more memories stick.

On the Saturday when Megatoad Stonie was giving himself stomach ache, and Alexis Sánchez was tucking away the penalty that sent a football-loving nation into celebrations, I was sitting on my bike on Bournemouth pier. It was day one of my twenty-eight-day journey. A massive storm the previous night had cleared the air perfectly, and I could not wait to get going. I say it was the start of the journey, but that is not strictly true. Like any great achievement, be it eating dozens of hotdogs consecutively, winning professional sporting competitions or anything else you might look back on in your life with pride, it was about more than just the day. My preparation for creating that memory and the many that would follow started around 18 months earlier.

I can't remember exactly where the idea came from. It may have been hatching in one form or another for years, but one day my crazy plan became a commitment (in my head at least). Indulge me here for a moment. Close your eyes and see if you can remember some of the crazy ideas you have had during the course of your life. Maybe you thought about taking a year out to travel the world. Learning to scuba dive or fly an aeroplane. Maybe writing a novel, perfecting another language, publishing your singing efforts on YouTube or developing an invention you've had in the back of your mind for years. Where are those ideas now? Do you know what stops people from pursuing their dreams? It's the absence of two things: personal commitment (believing you can and going for it) and sharing the idea with others (recognising that you will need support).

No matter how much you know or how talented you are, only commitment can turn opportunities and possibilities into been-there-done-that achievements. Regret must be one of the cruellest of emotions because it is attached to the past and things that only *could* have been. The beauty of the present is that it holds the keys to the future.

While I have your attention, I just wanted to say...

I've had hundreds of crazy ideas over the years, and I am proud of the fact that some of them are now my happiest memories. This particular triumph came about through a similar planning process to those I have used in previous attempts to discover my limit. I still don't know exactly where that bar stands, but I was confident this endeavour would get me far closer to finding out than anything I'd tried before. I've used the process in my work-life too, and it has served me well in growing my business, launching new products, planning activities, and persuading my wife I am not insane. My only slight concern is that by sharing the step-by-step detail here, she might be ready to put the breaks on the next time! But I'll take that risk. It works in four stages, like this:

HAVE AN IDEA. You cannot start a journey without having at least some idea of the destination, and what success looks like. The clearer you can be about what you want to achieve or the places you want to go, the better. But simply having a dream, ambition, or idea is a great place to start. It might be something as vague as a hike to Mount Everest base camp, organising a family reunion or starting a charity. Maybe even planting a dozen trees, learning to identify bird songs - or any one of the challenges I mentioned earlier. It makes no difference what it is; you just need a big idea. The key is to make it something that would mean a lot to you and fire up your sense of adventure or achievement. For me, the best ideas are those that make you feel a little bit (or even extremely) uncomfortable. If your idea doesn't stir something deep inside, it probably isn't big enough to change who you are.

CHECK FEASIBILITY. Please go through this stage *before* any financial outlay or committing too much time to pursuing your idea. You certainly want to tick this box before moving to stage three of the planning process. At the very least, it might avoid you looking silly or losing money you don't have. You need to confirm it is physically possible to do what you want to do. No matter what people say, there *are* limits to human achievement. I am all for dreaming big, and I would encourage anyone to push the boundaries of their ambitions because outside of the usual limitations is where the real fun, freedom and sense of being alive exists. You have to be realistic but do not ever let the fact that no one has done something (yet) stop you from being the first – someone has to be – why shouldn't it be you? If your ideas list includes things like running a three-and-a-half-minute mile, swinging between skyscrapers like Spiderman, or reversing the effects of climate change by next Christmas, you might be aiming a bit too high. But there may be achievable versions of those things you could try. I have always found that setting sights on goals beyond the realms of realism brings out the best in people and that even trying and failing is so much more exciting than sitting back and watching the world wander past. How will you know what is feasible if you don't try?

ANNOUNCE PUBLICLY. This is the big one. If you believe what you want to do might be achievable, even if no one else has ever even tried, and that you (with access to all the help you need) are the one to do it, just go ahead and try. Four things (in my experience) stop ideas from becoming real: your commitment, how much you want it, what it means to you—and letting yourself off the hook. By that, I mean not being answerable to other people for what you have decided you will do. For most people, once they have made their intentions public, it makes it doubly hard to go back on their word. So go and tell everyone.

PLAN METICULOUSLY. Once you have a realistic (exciting and limit-stretching, but ultimately doable) idea to pursue, you need a plan. The best-laid plans rarely stay the course of any adventure, but you still need to make one. Adjustments, tweaking, or a complete change of direction is inevitable, but the planning is still critical to your success. Plans always work best when you start at the end goals and work backwards to the present day. Questions like, 'what would have to happen for me to achieve this?' are often an excellent way to find the solution at each step.

There is a problem with meticulous planning, however, in that aiming for perfection is a sure way to stop action. You cannot start a big adventure or limit-stretching challenge by waiting until you are ready. That moment never comes because feeling underprepared is a natural defence mechanism built into our genome to help us survive. It is the very essence of adventure, and knowing it exists will help you find solutions beyond the plan. So, my plan, when I started out, was as meticulous as this:

I'm going to attempt a quadrathlon a day for 28 days while circum-navigating Great Britain!

So, there I was, one evening early in 2014, with a carefully selected group of friends around for dinner. I had gone through steps one and two of my tried and tested process and had arrived at stage three. The scene was set, and while Penny was a little suspicious at seeing the guest list (she had experienced this tactic before), I set myself to drop the bombshell. Perhaps it is strange for someone obsessed with pushing his physical and emotional thresholds to feel much more comfortable surrounded by backup when I announce these things.

Dinner was going well, and I sat there, eyeing the room and waiting for the right combination of wine consumption, light-heartedness and a suitable lull in the banter. The moment finally arrived, and slowly, trying desperately to balance childish excitement, grown-up credibility and wife-conscious reverence, I proceeded to share my plans. My friends know me well enough not to bother asking 'why' anymore, but Penny gave me that look, suggesting she would need a few more details this time. After the initial shocked silence, the mood was jubilant, and I quickly bagged my first volunteer, with my great friend Tim Mayes agreeing to accompany me for six days from Inverness to Scarborough.

Not surprised that I already had a costings spreadsheet, draft itinerary and pencilled-in route underway, Penny soon reverted to her amazing, supportive and superbly organised self. She set to work, helping me fine-tune the details and smooth through the trickier elements that I was struggling to quantify. As the news spread, other volunteers came forward and signed up to join in the fun (a day here, a few days there) or add a little support along the route. Various local businesses and people offered to sponsor aspects of the adventure, and, of course, The Pepper Foundation were behind me like a galeforce tailwind the entire way.

No drive = No destination

The idea that initially hatched in my mind 18 months earlier was set in stone long before I straddled my bike on that first Saturday in July 2015. There were times during the preparation stages when doubt set in, and a few obstacles seemed insurmountable as we talked through the planning. For example, the biggest setback was five weeks before the start of the challenge after I had attended a promotional event at our motorhome sponsor, Just Go. I was heading back down the M1 in galeforce winds when a huge crosswind ripped my kayak, bike, and the roof rack off my car and underneath the wheels of the lorry behind. Fortunately, no one was hurt, however with only five weeks to go, I now had no bike, and my kayak was damaged to the point where I didn't know if it was still seaworthy. At that point, although the challenge did look like it could be over before it had truly begun, there was no going back. We'll venture beneath the surface of our preparations later in the book, but let me leave you with this thought for now. Three things drove me, and each of them had become more important to me than the actual event itself.

UNSATISFIED LONGING. Something in me longs to know my limit – it is an insatiable urge. I know not everyone has this, but I do believe no one can achieve true fulfilment by living inside their comfort zone.

OTHER PEOPLE. After that deal-sealing dinner, I told everyone I met of my intentions. Most importantly, I hoped to raise a significant amount of money for The Pepper Foundation, and I was not about to let them down!

LIFE IS TOO SHORT. I don't mean to be agest, but (and this is generally true), if you are over forty, you will have realised that the years are flying by, and the fact that you are almost halfway to the UK's average life expectancy will not have passed your attention. (If reading the last sentence is the first time that dawns on you – sorry.) If you are below forty, although I think a large proportion of thirty-somethings could be in the former mindset too, you might still be under the illusion you have all the time in the world. Trust me – and if not me, wait until you have read some of the stories of children whose support is funded by The Pepper Foundation in later chapters. Life is preciously short.

I am even more aware of the shortness of life these days, and there is so much I want to do with mine; I simply do not have the time to wait for the right moment. Do you?

So they were my three biggest reasons to take on the challenge, and they continue to drive me today in everything I do. If there is one thing I want you to feel as you read this book, it is that time and life should be valued and not wasted. Take hold of the (sometimes uncomfortable) truth that every single day you are alive is precious, and be determined to live as many days as you can to the full!

In the next chapter, I will take you back to the 4th of July 2015. Not to a hotdog eating contest, a South American soccer stadium or an Independence Day parade, but an understated beachside send-off in Bournemouth and the start of twenty-eight days of beautifully hard work.

 DAY 2

Preparing for River Dart Swim

CHAPTER THREE

THE BIG DAY ARRIVES

I don't know who first coined the phrase, 'the first step is always the hardest', but I promise you it is complete nonsense. Ask any marathon runner, long-distance swimmer or person setting out to circumnavigate Great Britain on a bike, kayak and his own two arms and legs, and they will tell you the first step is easy. What is hard is dealing with the disappointment of being outdone by the weather, the emotional strain of not seeing your family for days, wrecking your tech, and battling enormous headwinds while peddling up a 1 in 4 gradient killer hill. And that was just in the first week. Trust me – 'the first step' was easy by comparison.

So, there I was, surrounded by the small group of family and friends who had journeyed to Bournemouth to see me set off. Other people were standing around, enjoying a casual day at the beach, and sending the occasional curious glance across at our discrete gathering. There were pictures to take and a few duties to fulfil with sponsors and supporters, but I just wanted to get going. The moment finally arrived, and eighteen months of scheming, dreaming, and meticulous planning became the first few pedals. And if that step was easy, there was nothing hard about my first 6km cycle ride down to the Sandbanks Ferry, either. It was a perfect way to gather the rush of emotions and childlike excitement of finally being underway. My good friend, Dave Roberts, the first of many who would accompany me on my epic adventure, kept pace and was under strict instructions not to set off too fast.

Let me clarify my earlier comments about 'first steps' for those who might still be arguing the case. I suppose the saying comes from the idea that most people don't even get started. Perhaps it is the fear of starting and failing or the enormity of the challenge which stops people from fulfilling their plans and dreams, but it seems to be a common disease. As you will see, during the pages of this book and on the days that followed this first step, there were challenges (you might even call them failures) along the way. I can't say I ever felt like giving up, but there were a few occasions where it wasn't much fun, and once or twice I let my imagination make a problem bigger than it actually was. (Sometimes it was the opposite, and the problem was bigger than I was prepared to admit – but that didn't stop me either.) So, the first step mattered, and if I hadn't completed that, I would not have accumulated a month of exciting memories to treasure.

It's not me; it's the others...

It was as we arrived at Sandbanks that the sight of my first kayak crossing came into view, showing off turbulent, taunting tidal waves; it was as though they were saying, "are you sure?" and Dave echoed the sentiment. He was only accompanying me in the cycling part of those first few days, and the expression on his face spoke far louder than his words. It would have looked like a broad smile of enjoyment to anyone else, but I knew Dave well, and I could tell what he was really thinking. That expression contained a multitude of complex emotions, from happiness and hope to concern, resignation, irony and a sprinkling of gallows humour. I'd seen that smile before on Dave's face and found it strangely reassuring. But I had been looking forward to this. And what others saw as a rough crossing just added to the excitement and anticipation bubbling under my skin. I caught Penny's eye too as the kayak hit the waves (my seeing-off party had followed me down by a car) and gave her a look to reassure her of my confidence, but I don't think she was buying it.

The rush of that first splash of salty water was incredible! At last, the plan felt alive, and I began creating some of those moments I had dreamed about for so long. It was me and the elements, my desire to push myself against the forces of nature (in this case, a wicked tide), and the thrill of the challenge. What should have been a 4km kayak turned out to be about 6km against a mighty headwind, but it was great to be underway and start fighting my way across to Knoll Beach.

We had an extended breakfast after the crossing, which was a mistake because it put me under pressure for the rest of the day (and those lessons kept coming throughout the month!). After the breakfast, it was back on the bike to Tyneham, and then my first run: a gentle, sun-blessed 9km trek around to beautiful Lulworth Cove. Dave pedalled alongside me, and a 100km cycle followed with him still questioning my sanity over the kayaking and the open water swim in store when we arrived at Exmouth Estuary. As the crow flies (or the fish swims), beach-to-beach, it is around 400 yards across to Dawlish Warren Spit. But with a 5-knot tidal current and the unknown element of tackling the first swim, my GPS recorded it as 1.5km before I finally reached the shore.

As I had descended into the water, a curious bystander turned to Richard Hillier (friend, logistics organiser and general superstar helper!) and said, "Does your mate know what he's doing?" to which Richard replied, "He seems to think he does". They both continued to watch in silence as I battled the tide and tried to avoid the shipping. In my mind, I was never in any danger, but I understand how it must have looked. An outside perspective can be invaluable and always worthy of being heard, but I also know that the person in the thick of the situation is the only one who truly knows how they feel.

Self-confidence is a rare and precious commodity and worth cultivating. It should not be confused with over-confidence, which is extremely dangerous. Self-confidence is built upon experience (knowing your limits), preparation (making sure you are ready) and bravery (going for it). If your ambition builds on that, and you can see the target clearer than anyone else, other people might question if you know what you are doing. By all means, listen to reason, but don't let anyone destroy your confidence in yourself.

Having reached the shore, totally exhilarated by the experience, I finished day one with another short run to Shaldon Strand. My simple dinner that evening had never tasted so good, and I slept deeply, ready for another early start.

Watch out for the jellyfish

I mentioned earlier how you make a plan with the expectation that it will need to change. But I had no idea how quickly a fundamental part of mine would need such a back-to-the-drawing-board, total rewrite.

The alarm rang out at 05:30 (its standard-setting for the rest of the challenge), and I was ready to go. The only difference between that morning and most of the following month was that I was sleeping in a real bed. We had booked into a B&B with my family, rather than the campervan where I would get my four and a half hours a night moving forward.

After waving goodbye to Penny and the kids, Dave and I got on our bikes and headed off to Dartmouth on a 32km cycle to start the day. We arrived on the east side of the ferry crossing and packed Dave and the bikes onto the van and ferry before preparing for the swim. When the ferry captain realised what I was about to do, he matter-of-factly said, “Watch out for the jellyfish”.

A few strokes in, I realised what he meant. The channel was full of magnificent, translucent creatures, each one the size of a golf umbrella but without a colourful logo. While it was initially a surprise, I knew they were relatively harmless (to my wetsuit at least), and they were oblivious to me, effortlessly propelling themselves through the dark water in whatever direction they happened to be facing.

The fascinating smack of jellyfish was just another object to avoid as I swam across the busy waterway, looking out for boats and beasts as I went. In all, it was a thoroughly enjoyable swim and a great way to assure me that my training had been on point as I got into the rhythm of day two. But as I left the water to prepare for the next stage, the realisation came crashing down that my technical planning had not been as thorough as my physical preparation.

Too many transitions spoil the task

There were just too many transitions. I also over-anticipated my cycling speed and hadn’t allowed enough time for breaks, food, photos and trips to the bushes (or pub WCs). Constantly going from bike to kayak to running shoes to swimmers and back to the bike was complicated, tiring and time-consuming. Add to this a bit of confusion with the support team about the best time to be packed up for the night, and I realised I would need to adjust – big time. So, instead of precisely following the twenty-eight-day schedule I had been working on for over a year, I began replanning and reshaping the next day at the end of the current one. Each evening I sat down with my maps and notes to set out the new details of the following day before even thinking about sleep.

I love a challenge, physical or mental, so this added an extra dimension to the adventure, and there was no way I was going to be defeated. I think it was then that I realised that, for me, the undertaking was never about the achievement. It was the *doing* which inspired me: living in the moment, dealing with the situation at hand and rising to the challenge. I guess it taught me that if you only ever live for the destination, you miss out on so much of the rich experiences involved in getting there. But living in the moment, under the pressure of an extreme physical or mental challenge, forces you to be 100% focused on that moment. The truly wonderful thing about this is the escape it gives you from the mundaneness of everything else in your life. With every ounce of your attention focused on peddling into a gale-driven headwind, fighting waves, or simply staying alive, you become supremely aware of the preciousness of time. Of course, you cannot stay in moments like that forever, but the more you take hold of, the stronger your appreciation of life will become.

The incredible modern world with all its comforts and technology does come with a downside because it overloads our brains with distractions and unnecessary stresses. Adventures take us back to how we are meant to be: concentrating on life's key fundamentals. And I promise you the result is liberating and rewarding.

The rest of day two involved three more 50km cycles, two short swims and a couple of kayak crossings (you can see why I had to change the format). But it was the kayak across Plymouth Sound to Cremyll I remember the most. It was ferocious!

No matter how much you've seen, read or learned from other people's experiences, nothing can prepare you for doing it yourself. I was ready for headwinds and harsh tidal currents; I'd trained for them and faced them before. But looks can be deceiving too, and as I launched the kayak into the water, it looked magnificent. The sun shone, the sea glimmered, and the scene was well and truly set. I hadn't ventured far before the resistance appeared in full force. A crossing that should have taken just over an hour took two and a half, as a relentless barrage of wave upon wave warned me to stay away from Cremyll and shouted, "you shall not pass".

I have a treasured picture I took halfway across. Its value is not because it is beautiful, but because it cost me 30 metres of seriously hard graft. And if I took a drink or eased the pace of the paddle for even a moment, the sea pushed me backwards without care. Finally, however, I arrived, breathless and full of victorious exhilaration, safe on the Cremyll side of The Sound.

As with the route planning difficulties, challenges like kayaking across Plymouth Sound are a great reminder that the initial plan matters but is rarely perfect. You simply don't know what the next corner or wave will bring, so you have to be dynamic, resourceful and determined enough to go ahead and succeed anyway. It's the only way to get through life's many turns, transitions and storms.

Day two ended with another significant plan failure. And this one involved that all-important commodity 'food', but I'll share that story with you in the next chapter.

 DAY 3

St Mawes

Lands End

St Ives

Crossing Plymouth Sound

CHAPTER FOUR

THE HIGHS AND LOWS OF LIFE

Days three and four arrived in complete contrast to one another and left me with a profound truth I have pondered from time to time ever since: frustration is more exhausting than exhaustion is frustrating. It is a common theme in life, but we don't always consider or appreciate the difference. What sort of day would you prefer? Slow-paced and frustrating or hard yards and rewarding? For me, there is not even a debate, as the next two days will prove.

The third day was bound to get a little emotional because it began without my family, who I had watched return to ordinary life without me for a while the night before. To mark the occasion, we had booked our evening dinner at The Rising Sun in St Mawes (one of the Brash clan's favourite places for a family meal whenever we are in Cornwall). We had also agreed to do some promotional photos with sponsors and the pub's owners, so it was more than just a sentimental stop. But the delays and circumstances caused by too many transitions that day, and compounded by the incompetent farce of a local taxi company, meant we had to make do with 'homemade' in the support vehicle. I had already decided a daily re-plan to reduce the number of changeovers was necessary, but this episode confirmed it would have to become an essential part of my routine.

Every journey will be a mixture of highs and lows to enjoy or endure. Interestingly, for me, missing dinner with my family that night was more of a low than some of the physically and emotionally challenging days to come. I suppose it was the idea that months of planning and lots of promises could so easily come to nothing – over seemingly nothing.

With obligation in mind, and because we were still keen to catch up with friends, we started day three with a slight detour on our first cycle and had breakfast in The Rising Sun instead (ironically, just minutes after the sun had risen). It was good to see the place again, thank the Cornish Brewery for their support, and take a few 'pint in hand' photographs outside for the record (albeit a for-show-only breakfast pint). Although it just wasn't quite the same without Penny and the children enjoying one of our favourite places to visit and eat together.

Planning has to be dynamic

The key lesson here is that change is inevitable, and the test of a good plan is how it reacts to circumstances. If I were to attempt the challenge again and punctiliously access every lesson from each hour of the entire twenty-eight days, accounting for every single planning issue or unexpected twist we encountered, other things would go wrong. It doesn't matter how often you do the same thing, always expect the unexpected. A good plan has to be dynamic, and if you make plans with the certainty of uncertainty in mind, you will always be in the best place to manage when calamity calls.

The next planned part of day three was a 6km kayak across Falmouth Harbour. I was super excited but a 25-mile-per-hour headwind soon stopped my childlike exuberance for adventure. I had discussed with Penny that if there were ever a marginal decision regarding safety, I would err on the side of caution. Marginal is, of course, a broad and relatively subjective concept, but on this occasion, I made the same choice she would have enforced. After all, I'd promised her I wouldn't kill myself on the journey (and she would have killed me if I'd broken that promise this early in the challenge).

My wise decision resulted in an extended detour on the bike, culminating in a 130km cycle to Land's End. It was an enjoyable experience but still tinged with angst because it put all my timings out again. Dave was still with me, so it was nice to get out on the road again with him and take out my frustration on the pedals. There was no easing off the pace this time, as I had a heartful of latent irritation to release.

I was met with an odd and entirely unexpected emotion when we arrived at Land's End. The last time I was there, it was something of a victory, having just completed an 850 mile cycle from John o'Groats. It was merely a pit stop on a much larger endeavour this time. Having missed my first kayak that day, I was looking forward to the second one, and it came at the end of a reprise from the morning's disruptions via a tailwind cycle to St Ives in bright sunshine. Whereas the cancelled one would have been tough, even in safe conditions, this one was supposed to be easy. It was 8km across to Godrevy Beach, and the first 98% went according to plan. Then disaster struck. Again.

As I was paddling to the shore, I lost concentration for a moment as a big wave sideswiped me into the blue. I was in the shallows and quickly managed to right the kayak and paddle the last few yards, but my kit (including phone, GPS and SatNav) were soaked through and ruined. To paint the analogy a little clearer, I was on the crest of a wave, well above troubled waters, enjoying the sunshine, almost across the line, then taken off guard and capsized. This time it wasn't the plan that had failed me; it was a lapse in concentration. It was as though I had walked into the oldest con in the book: frustration, followed by fair weather, allowing a distraction and... boom. Challenges are called challenges for a reason, and you cannot afford to take your eye off the goal just because the going is good.

For the rest of the month (remember, this is just day three), I had to rely on my backup kit, including second rate tech and slower connection speeds. This was another complication on what was turning out to be the sort of day I really had not planned for so early in the adventure. The day ended with a run and another short cycle ride through Padstow, finally arriving for dinner in Rock.

The ironman, the foodie and the driving rain

If yesterday had been frustrating, day four was, by complete comparison, just plain hard. But I loved it! That was what I had planned to face. We spent the night in the support vehicle, in a Brit Stop pub car park, The Ring O'Bells in St Issey, and set off at 6 am on a 100km cycle, with a 3km running interlude. This was Dave's last day, and an adventurous friend of a friend, Alex, who works for the RNLI (Royal National Lifeboat Institution) and was in training for a Half Ironman, also joined us for the day. That morning turned out to be the wettest morning of the entire twenty-eight days (even though I couldn't have been further from Scotland), so it was good to have someone so experienced at saving people from drowning alongside.

We arrived in Appledore for our kayak ride and met up with Radio Two's food expert, my good friend Nigel Barden. He was giving out an award in the area and, already a keen supporter and promotor of our efforts, gave us a 'shout out' on the Radio to help raise a few more pounds. It was great to see his familiar face at that point in the day, especially as this would be my first lone section of the challenge. Alex had to cycle back to Padstow for work the following morning, and Dave was going home.

As if in response to the warmth and high spirits generated by Nigel and his BBC audience, the weather decided to switch modes and share some sunshine. In keeping with the sudden brightness, the launch into the River Taw was perfect, and it was nothing short of an idyllic paddle as I made my way upstream along the smaller River Caen and arrived at Broughton Pil. The gentle, lonely, 8km kayak was peace and reflection personified and a lovely way to get me ready for the trial that awaited me at the end. I even had time to apply a little sunscreen.

The big climb and the return of the rain!

So far, so good. The weather had been playing games all morning, but the plan was intact, and the pain to come was what I had signed up for. I set off alone on the bike for the first time in four days, off to face the Goliath that stood tall and defiantly before me. Exmoor National Park is home to the notorious 1-in-4 gradient Countisbury Hill, and I was relishing the battle for supremacy and height. These sorts of ascents are all about exploring pain and keeping going regardless of every fibre in your body shouting at you to stop. Ironically, I have always found the effort to be the best way to chase away the tiredness of previous excursions. My body was full of questions after three and a half days of physical and emotional effort, angst and readjustment, but I had determined I would be in control of the answers.

Fear of hard work is a disadvantage in life for two reasons. Firstly, it means you cannot escape the bounds of ordinary and plain sailing because life is just not that simple. Anything worth having almost always comes with a cost, which usually translates into hard work. Secondly, without testing yourself, you never learn anything. Yes, some people are born wealthy, lucky or privileged and never have to work for anything in life. But I pity those people. Because, potentially, the shallowness of their experience results in a lack of growth and learning opportunities. I believe the joy of life comes from the challenges it presents or those we choose to face.

The secret to surviving tough times and hard work is knowing a future exists where you will be able to stop, enjoy the view and freewheel for a while. That knowledge is often the result of past experiences, combined with detailed planning and confidence in how life works (making allowances for the unexpected).

Arriving at the top of Countisbury Hill, Exmoor, was a wonderful moment (although I had been physically sick just before the peak), and the solitary selfie I took there holds more emotional value than anyone else could know. As I sipped my energy drink at the top, enjoying the view and waiting for my heartbeat to regain its composure, the expectation sent it spinning again. Because, as with any ascent, the offer of a freewheel follows. And, to add to the thrill, the threat of spill and the wind-defying buzz of the descent, my old friend, the driving rain, returned. It was exhilarating, and at one point, the GPS on my bike displayed just over 90km per hour. Stupidly fast and stupendously good fun!

It's all downhill from here on

It's all downhill from here on. I know I mentioned this phrase earlier and attempted to analyse it. But I'm revisiting it once more (bear with me) because, well, it fascinates me. On the one hand, it implies you've hit the high spot, and things will never be that good again. Or it could refer to the idea that you have overcome a test or trial or have the wisdom of maturity, and things are about to get a whole lot easier. I like to think I am a combination of realist and optimist and favour the latter definition, seeing each challenge as a milestone reached and an opportunity to take that momentum into the next one. Sometimes it does feel as if life is one struggle after another, but even then, I think that makes those speedy downhills even more worthwhile. My point is that how you see life's ups and downs is a decision *you* get to take. Circumstances are often out of our control, but how we face them is always a choice.

The Pepper Foundation is a place where children and their families have to face these decisions each day. It exists to provide free home care and support to help alleviate the suffering of children with complex health needs or life-limiting conditions. Those children did not ask to be ill; they are not there through a misdemeanour or by any fault of their own. For them, life is a series of uphill struggles, and there is rarely a picturesque view or sun-soaked backdrop to ease the pain. But I promise you they value the little blessings along the way: the freewheels, the celebrations, the breakthroughs and the chance to get out and live and love a little more, a little longer.

Don't worry; this is not 'the interlude' where I ask you to put down the book and call a freephone number with your card details (although there is an email for Pepper at the back of the book if you want to donate or help). Rather, this is where I want you to stop and see how you choose to view the ebbs and flows in your life. Seriously – take a moment, right now.

Day four ended with an unpleasant sewage infested swim at Burnham on Sea, but the less said about that, the better! And another supportive friend, Simon Cole, joined me that evening, bringing my first lone adventuring day to an end. I'll introduce you to him in the next chapter.

DAY 4

Appledore

Countisbury Hill

Burnham on Sea

CHAPTER FIVE

GET USED TO LIVING IN THE MOMENT

When you are doing a twenty-eight-day challenge to circumnavigate England, Scotland and Wales, you learn fairly quickly that you can only tackle one day at a time. You cannot get a head start on day nineteen's swim during day seven or let a decision you made on day three affect your choices on day five. What's happened cannot be unhappened. What is done is done, and what is due to be done tomorrow cannot be done today. Yes, you can plan ahead and learn from what is passed, and you absolutely should, but you can only *actually* do anything in the present day.

So, I could not let what I described as a marginal decision at Falmouth Harbour a couple of days earlier affect my judgment regarding today's dilemma. Today (day five) was supposed to be the big kayak: the one I had been looking forward to long before I decided to embark on this challenge—16 km across the Severn Estuary, from Weston Super Mare to Swanbridge Bay near Barry. But the horrendously stormy weather from yesterday showed no signs of relent, and even to the most optimistic mind, marginal seemed like a generous description of my choice this time. It was treacherous. As we looked across the water and the storm of six-foot-high white horses galloping down the channel, chased by angry galeforce winds, it was clear the crossing could not happen. And yet...I pondered the possibility.

Maybe it was the disappointment of the Falmouth cancellation and the frustration that followed, or just that I had dreamed about this crossing for so long. Whatever it was, I stood there for quite some time, straining to find a good reason to do the utterly unreasonable. Simon waited patiently for me to accept the only correct decision, and my emotions finally stood down and allowed me to rethink. The day before had been physically challenging, and the added emotional disappointment at not attempting the crossing took its toll. Without thinking, I took my eye off the timing ball again and gave in to the temptation of a consolatory cooked breakfast before heading to Barry in the motorhome. And as I finished that final mouthful of bacon and eggs, my energy just disappeared.

I had made this day shorter on purpose, knowing Exmoor would be a challenge, but it still caused no end of issues, and maybe, in retrospect, it should have been easier still. But I was there at that moment, and there was nothing I could do but face its demands. I could not redo the previous day or tackle the next, but one thing was absolutely certain: the challenge would be over before I got there if I didn't find a way through this one.

We were over an hour behind an already tight schedule by the time we set off on the bikes from Barry. And though we faced the same ferocious westerly headwind that had made the water impassable, getting back in the saddle had resurrected my resolve. We had agreed to stop in at the Tredz Giant Bike Store in Swansea to meet the sponsors who had supplied my bike. This was 100% needed, as the whole reason I was there was to raise money for Pepper, but it felt like an unnecessary and unwelcome distraction at the time. I smiled through the (what seemed at the time) irrelevant tea, cakes, photos, and small talk, but I could not wait to get going again.

Note: If the wonderful and generous people from Tredz are reading this book and thought I seemed a little off that day – now you know why! Apologies, and thank you for your amazing support.

At last, Simon and I were back with the day's calling and continued to fight the wind as we made our way west towards Pembroke. But the tiredness was creeping in again, and it attacked full-on by the end of the day. I worked out later that we had wasted three to four hours through poor judgement and obligations that day. And, around 20km short of my intended destination, I collapsed. Hypothermia set in from the weather (and no doubt the stress), and my imagination started running away with the idea that I had ruined the challenge before I'd barely begun.

Jonathan Tweed from The Pepper Foundation joined us for dinner that evening, and alongside Simon's positivity, his morale boost refocused my mind on why I was there. While still feeling a little weak, I put on a brave face and just listened to the others laugh, smile, talk about the Foundation's work, and recap on the first week's adventures. And it didn't take long to start feeling better. A huge curry helped too, and my recovery was well on the way before I fell into a deep and refreshing sleep that night.

Often in life, especially when plans fail, circumstances seem stacked against you. Your stride is interrupted, and overwhelm sets in; it is tempting to take the easy way out. In my experience, this is almost always an emotional trap rather than a real one. Whatever comes against you, no matter how hard, usually all you need to do is find some friends and just survive the day because you cannot tell how things will look by the morning – I'll wager they will usually feel a whole lot better.

Speculation, anticipation, preconception and exceeding expectation

So, I woke up that morning with one solitary thought in my mind: today. The day before had been a complete nightmare, but I am writing that now in retrospect. As I prepared myself to face day six, I did not give day five a moment's thought. Drifting off the night before, I had decided only a fool would choose to take a defeatist attitude into the following day. Treat each day as a new one, build on your victories, learn from tough experiences and determine that you will give it your very best. To approach any day with any other mindset is akin to a football team turning up to a match and offering their opponents a two-nil lead before kick-off.

My 'waking up' took place early and in the campervan, parked in the aptly named Speculation Inn, Hundleton, Pembrokeshire. I was looking forward to and expecting a great day. All the feelings of disappointment, exhaustion and wanting to give up were filed away as experience, and nothing was going to get in the way of today's adventure.

It was a sunny morning, and as if in response to my new-day-new-start mindset, we were gifted a welcome tailwind for the first leg. My body was still in recovery mode, but my thoughts were focused, and I couldn't wait to get going, come what may. Simon and I set off on the bikes and, despite initially taking a wrong turning that sent us over a mile in the wrong direction, we were soon well on our way to St Davids.

Preconceptions can often surprise you

Starting with the right attitude quickly paid dividends, and after a great breakfast in St Davids, the sun still shone, as if wishing us well while we turned the corner and headed north along the glorious Welsh coastline. Now, picture the trading port of Fishguard in your mind for a moment. When I planned the trip and saw the name on the map, it barely registered as any more than a passing road sign. If I had thought about it at all, I would have probably imagined a run-of-the-mill, functional, nothing-to-see-here, dull, colourless and featureless fishing town. It is certainly not mentioned on any tourist leaflet I have ever seen. But how wrong you can be if you rely on preconceptions. Fishguard is, without doubt, one of the prettiest little seaside towns I have ever encountered and a real gem; hidden away just below the Pembrokeshire Coast National Park. I was just glad we passed through on a day when my mind was in the right place because had I been feeling sorry for myself like the day before, I might have missed out on recognising its charms. Isn't it amazing what a change in perspective can do for your vision?

We carried on past Aberystwyth, enjoying the sunny disposition, clear blue skies and sea views to rival any coastline, anywhere in the world. Wales truly is beautiful. With around 170km on the bikes behind us that day, we arrived at Borth for a gentle 5km run and then enjoyed a swim across the river mouth at Aberdovey.

Simon did not consider himself a strong swimmer and was not keen on the crossing at first. But in contrast to the previous day, we had made good time, so we sat down in front of the water to talk it through while eating ice cream (my only one of the entire journey). It didn't take too much persuasion in the end and always being up for a challenge, he decided to push his boundaries and join me in the fresh, calm, jellyfish-infested waters. As he exited on the other side, the smile on his face said it all. Challenges can be daunting; I suppose that's why they are called challenges, but overcoming them is the sweetest savour of all.

As I write this, thinking about the contrast between days five and six, it occurs to me that real issues affected the decisions and actions I took. Circumstances beyond my control were at play, and it would have been impossible to stick to the exact route and activities I had mapped out all those months before. That is life in a nutshell. The real difference was nothing to do with what the elements presented me with; it was my perspective and attitude that determined how those days transpired.

As you will see in chapter eight, the life of a child supported by The Pepper Foundation is entirely different to that of an average child living in ordinary circumstances. I don't want to generalise too much, and I know that life can be tough for everyone. We all have to deal with hardships, losses, and broken hearts from time to time, and The Pepper Foundation certainly doesn't have a monopoly on looking after people with needs. But when you consider the perspective of waking up in the morning as a child, knowing you have a life-limiting condition and not being able to do anything about it, the reality becomes daunting. Compare that to waking up with the usual troubles of growing up in mind, but the expectation of a long life ahead. It does make you think, doesn't it? As I share more of my adventures, I hope that introducing you to some of the remarkable children who have turned the less fortunate circumstances delivered them into a fulfilled life helps build your appreciation, just as it has mine.

When you look at situations with a greater perspective, full of thanks for the opportunities you have and determined not to let yesterday's disasters affect today, it tends to improve your starting position. That start does not always mean you will win, but that doesn't matter because you can reset and start again the next day.

After Simon and I emerged from the refreshing swim across to Aberdovey's northern shore, we got back on the bikes for a short cycle ride to Fairbourne. From there, it was a delightful kayak finish crossing from Fairbourne to Barmouth, where my brother, Tony, was waiting on the beach to lead us to a few beers and a fish and chip supper. A perfect way to finish what had been a reaffirming and strength-enhancing day.

DAY 6

Borth Beach

St Davids

Barmouth Beach

CHAPTER SIX

GOOD FRIENDS, NEW FRIENDS, A PERFECT DAY AND REFLECTION

Day six had reminded me of a fundamental principle I had learned so many years before. Maybe it is a symptom of being human that makes us so vulnerable to forgetting what we already know. That is why I have always chosen to push myself beyond where I feel comfortable. To remind me of the things I have learned before and give myself every opportunity to reinforce hard-won truths and discover even more.

I don't particularly believe in fate. My experience tells me that the rough and the smooth arrive indiscriminately, and there is little you can do to change it. But, as I explained in the last chapter, you have complete control over how you handle what comes your way. In all areas of life, I have found it is best to take the rough and look forward to the smooth. So, when day seven delivered the perfect conditions for one of the highlights of the entire adventure, I was ready to make the most of the day.

Day seven marked the end of the first quarter of the whole challenge and would also be the only time I had to complete seven days continuously. As it turned out, I couldn't have picked a more majestic and memorable way to mark the occasion – it was spectacular. If I had been disappointed at missing out on my kayak across the Severn Estuary, I was overjoyed at the more than perfect conditions the Menai Straits had in store for me later that day.

However, we still had a few miles to get through before arriving at that great expectation. After leaving the campsite in Barmouth, Simon and I set off on the bikes and unexpectedly crossed paths with a bubbly cyclist, Paula, who was out training for an Ironman competition, and her joyful company for a few miles was a great way to start the day. Arriving at Royal St Davids Golf Club in Harlech, we had a lovely run along the beach, decorated by a stunning backdrop with the majestic peak of Mount Snowdon at its centre. I persuaded Simon to join me for another short swim at the end of the beach as we passed Clough Williams-Ellis's Portmeirion, and then we tucked into a few bacon butties for breakfast.

Getting to know other travellers along Lon Eifion's journey

It was then back on the bikes and along the magical Lon Eifion Cycleway through Porthmadog to Caernarfon. Even on a lonely day, this trek would stir the emotions and whisper fairy tales to those who passed by; but on bustle-filled days, its charms truly come to life. We enjoyed the latter, and it seemed that every few miles, we would stop to mingle with school parties, family outings, day-trippers, adventurers and those, like us, on charitable quests. This time of shared passion for life, sunshine, and the great outdoors made it one of the most wonderful sections of the journey to that point, but the best was just about to start. It is a reminder that while we all live within the confines of our own mind and body, it is the connections we have with other people trekking the wilds of life's journey that make it such a meaningful and worthwhile pursuit.

Menai delivers, memories are made, and Richard says farewell...

Picture the scene: a golden sun, glimmering in the richest of Welsh blue skies, the perfect tide, a gentle cooling breeze, launching the kayak at the base of the imposing, impressive Caernarfon Castle and paddling into the Menai Straits. Of all the days, moments, trails and waterways I had planned for this trip, this was always going to be a high point. And it didn't disappoint! For seventeen glorious kilometres of smooth delight, Simon and I had the tide on our side and the sun shining its approval. We shared the experience for a few minutes with Richard and Tony, who waved and shouted from the famous Menai Bridge as we passed underneath. Even the white water 'swellies' were kind enough to invite us to pass through with their blessing and barely more than a friendly splash and a wave.

As we emerged from the dreamlike waters at Bangor, Simon cut his foot quite badly on the barnacle-infested slipway. I have a great photo of him smiling broadly with his foot over the blood-soaked kayak, reminiscent of the famous scene from my favourite film, Jaws. After patching him up and feeling almost as if we had gone back in time for a few hours and now safely returned, it was back on the bikes for the final leg of the perfect day. Chris Kelsey, a friend from our main sponsor, The Marble and Granite Centre, had driven all the way from Newcastle just to say 'hello' at Bangor: another surprise moment that helped make the day such a highlight.

That kayak was a memory that will always bring a smile to my mind, and it was made far more valuable to have shared it with Simon. I owed him that much for having forced him on a few swims previously, although I know he secretly enjoyed those too. And of all the days in my month-long adventure, this one totally delivered.

The cycle around the top of North Wales took us away from the Anglesey coastline, west through Llandudno, Colwyn Bay, and Rhyl, then over the border back into England. A day that had promised to be amazing (then over-delivered in spades) ended in West Kirby with a touch of sadness – but no regret.

My very good friend, Richard Hillier, had been my backup support for the full seven days, and it was now time to say goodbye. He had been a rock and the main constant up to that point. Richard is a phenomenal organiser, and with his positive outlook on life and willingness to roll his sleeves up, I could not have hoped for anyone better to help get my challenge off to a strong start. The rest of the adventure would be different without him. But as is so often the case in life, I didn't realise quite how much it would change things. And as the next few lonely days would teach me, you can't overestimate the power of friendship and support, and you only really know how much it means to you when it's no longer at your side.

DAY 7

Harlech Beach

Menai Straits

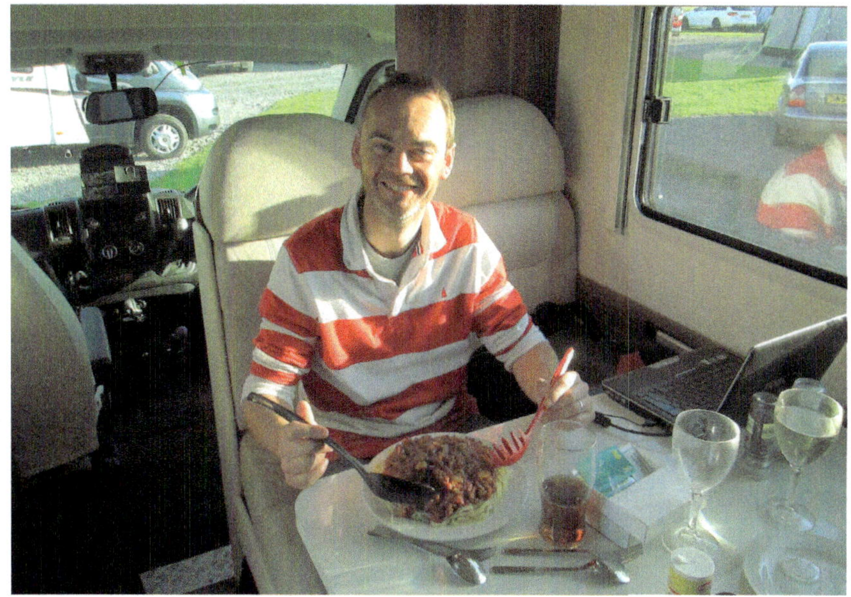

Wales

Royal St Davids Golf Club

CHAPTER SEVEN

LIFE IS LIKE A PARTY BALLOON

You will have noticed The Pepper Foundation's party balloon branding on the cover of this book and the introduction from Pat Daley, the Chair of The Pepper Foundation, at the start. And there is every chance you purchased your copy of this book at one of their events. I have also explained earlier how my twenty-eight-day journey was to scratch a gigantic itch in my thirst for adventure, search out my limits, and raise money and awareness for the Foundation. In the next chapter, I want to introduce you to Aayushi and Max and share their extraordinary stories of hope, endurance and living life to the full. Before we get there, I will explain one of the personal philosophies that drives me to do the kind of things you're reading about in this book.

To me, life is like a party balloon, not unlike the pink, heart-shaped one that sits alongside Pepper's logo. It symbolises celebration, love and recognition of reaching a target or goal. And every time I experience a day like the one I described in chapter six, it feels like I am sending a big, bright and lively breath of air into my party balloon. As a result, my life looks and feels a little fuller, bolder, and bursting with more energy than it did the day before.

In my imagination, everyone is born with their own party balloon attached to their heart, but at birth, it is newly out of the packet, awaiting to receive its first puff of air. As babies, we experience new things every day. Our first smile, first gurgle, first words, first crawl, first step. Each of these new experiences adds a puff of air to our balloon, and in our early years, there are so many new experiences that our party balloon quickly begins to inflate. And as we develop into toddlers, we try new experiences every day, unencumbered by fear of failure or embarrassment.

But as we approach double-digits, our brains, bodies and awareness develop. We understand more about the world around us, and we start to learn the connection between risk and the potential for pain. This leads to mental barriers forming every time we face new experiences or challenges. Sometimes these barriers are not even created by our own experiences but by the fears, prejudice and opinions of our parents, teachers, or friends. Fear of the dark, fear of spiders, fear of heights, fear of water and fear of pretty much anything else is a learned behaviour, not one we were born with. For example, my children's fear of wasps is not as a result of them being stung many times by the amazing little insects but instead from seeing the reaction of others when the flying creatures visit our summer BBQ dinners: the unwarranted hysteria really is something to see, and I find it hilarious.

Perhaps the biggest enemy of the party balloon is a child's teenage years, where the fear of embarrassment amongst your peers becomes all-encompassing and, for some, totally debilitating. This is where the reluctance to step outside their comfort zone (socially, physically and mentally) becomes set in stone for many people. From my work with young people over the years, I have seen first-hand how this can result in countless missed opportunities in a young life. But the saddest thing is that the neural pathways of fear laid out in childhood are why so many people settle for lives that are run-of-the-mill and void of adventure in adulthood.

In this metaphor, each fear acts like a tiny pinprick in the skin of the balloon, letting out a small puff of air. When we are young, this does not have a huge impact on the volume of the balloon as the leaking air is far outweighed by the new experiences and an unbridled willingness to step outside our comfort zone. The balloon continues to grow, protected by our adolescent, seemingly indestructible bodies and minds viewing life through the prism of immortality. I have always found it fascinating that, as children, we are under the illusion that we have all the time in the world until we reach a mysterious age where we start to notice the years flying by.

As we move through to middle age, we settle into the groove of working life, purposely trying to find ways of making life easier and less challenging. And with dependent families growing around us, stepping out of our comfort zones brings a level of risk that we tend to avoid at all costs. Consequently, inflating our party balloon (in my mind, the very essence of life) with new challenges and experiences becomes harder and less frequent as our fears increase, putting more pinpricks in the balloon each day. Eventually, our party balloon begins to shrink instead of inflating, as the occasional puffs are not enough to replace the ever-increasing pinpricks of air leaking out.

When you think about party balloons, there is surely no sadder sight than a soft, saggy one lying forgotten; leaking air on the floor of a celebration that never quite got going because most guests had better things to do that day.

But all is not lost. I believe that it does not take a lot of effort to keep your party balloon from getting to this state. All you need to do is keep challenging yourself to do things outside your comfort zone. Learn new skills, experience new places, sights, food, events, adventures, and overcome fears. It is never too late to repair the holes in your party balloon, and there are always opportunities to keep inflating it by replacing your 'why' with 'why not'? Face your fears and live as much as possible outside your comfort zone; trust me, it is much more fulfilling and fun!

Now, let's meet some children and their parents whose balloons you could never describe as half-full or deflated.

CHAPTER EIGHT

MEET AAYUSHI AND MAX

Aayushi's story

I am writing this chapter in the second half of 2021, shortly after seventeen months of various levels of lockdown in the UK caused by the COVID-19 pandemic. Regardless of what happens in the future, concerning that or other challenges facing the world, it is fair to say it affected everybody's life more than we could have imagined. But it was potentially more traumatic for those who were already carrying far greater burdens and responsibilities than most. Having said that, my observation has often been that people who bear much can cope with more. Resilience is a hard-won but powerful tool to have in your personal armoury.

Aayushi has a severe Neuro-disability, and over the years, her mother Shambhavi and their family have relied on help from various services to look after Aayushi's needs. For families in these situations, as you can imagine, routine and regular contact is a critical aspect in maintaining a secure, happy and healthy living environment. To add to the concern of services being put on hold as the full extent of the pandemic was starting to dawn on the world, Aayushi suddenly became very ill. And as she approached her eighteenth birthday in March 2020, it increasingly looked like she would not survive long enough to see a milestone that most teenagers take for granted.

Shambhavi said, *'At the beginning of lockdown when Aayushi was very poorly, and we were quarantined, I was concerned that nobody would be coming into our home and that we would not have the support we needed. It felt like there were a lot of things going on and we were feeling overwhelmed with all the different discussions about her deteriorating condition'.*

Through a series of conversations with specialist nurses at the Children's Hospice at Home who already had first-hand knowledge and understanding of Aayushi's condition, they created a care plan that reflected the family's needs.

'Having the nurses at this time, when Aayushi was at her most vulnerable, gave us great peace of mind', Shambhavi explained. *'It was quickly recognised we were looking after a very ill child with complex needs, and the Children's Hospice at Home nurses coordinated with the community nurses and other teams to put together a support plan. The nurses were on-hand in the evenings and weekends, which was a big relief for me as I did not want Aayushi to go to the hospital or see an out-of-hours GP as they don't know her well enough.'*

No one can push through on their own

As you can imagine, life can be challenging under normal circumstances. But with a severe Neuro-disability, plus the added pressure of any support being limited to phone calls and the usual team of nurses and support staff unable to visit Aayushi, the uncertainty increased. This is where clear and concise communication becomes essential. While I was on my journey around the British coastline and on any other adventure I have undertaken, the support team and communication have been critical. Even in those moments where I have felt very alone (as you will read about in the next chapter), just the knowledge that people who love me were out there somewhere made all the difference. As you read the rest of Aayushi's story, maybe think about those in your life who might need a bit of reassurance that you care. You never know what a phone call might do to change or make a day.

Shambhavi described one occasion during a lockdown period where Aayushi started behaving strangely. The family could not work out if it was the side effects of the medication she'd been given or if something else was bothering her. They called their GP, who advised going to the hospital. But the family were very nervous about exposing her to COVID-19 while potentially sitting for hours in what was, at the time, a seriously overburdened NHS. So, before setting off with an impending sense of dread at the unknown, they called Leanne, a Clinical Nurse Specialist, who was very familiar with their situation. Leanne listened carefully, reassured the family it was not a side effect of the medication but another cause and gave them some instructions to help. Although the nursing team couldn't enter the home, Shambhavi found the service provided on the phone reassuring. From then on, they were available on the phone at any time, even out-of-hours, offering advice on Aayushi's symptoms, including the proper medication to manage her pain, and discussed issues with the GP to make sure the best advice was given.

Shambhavi said, *'It was a really, really, really brilliant experience, and I was so happy that Aayushi had the Children's Hospice nurses looking after her. They even had conversations on our behalf so that I didn't need to manage the handovers between different teams, as I was finding it so overwhelming at the time'.*

Reflecting on the family's experience during lockdown, Shambhavi told me they had started with increased levels of fear and anxiety about how they would get through. From the first week, when they thought they would lose their daughter, just weeks before she would celebrate a milestone birthday, and through many other occasions where the pressure was mounting. But through compassion, communication and expert care, a team of amazing nurses and support workers, backed by funding from charities like The Pepper Foundation, turned a tragedy into a triumph. Aayushi had a fabulous birthday party - with lots of balloons! Her family have many photos from that special day and memories that will live long in their hearts and lives. And she continues to light up the house with her smiles and appreciation of every day, especially those days when her heroes, the nurses who support her wellbeing, come and visit.

Asked about her overall experience during what looked like a very dark time in the family's lives, Shambhavi said, *'It feels like we experienced both sides of the coin as when my daughter was really poorly, and we didn't think she would make her birthday, being in lockdown made the situation much worse. The high level of support was not something I was expecting at all, and it was great to see the nurses coming together with the consultant and GP to make a plan for how we could look after Aayushi at home'.*

Max's story

I found Max's story particularly pertinent to this book because it is all about determination to do your best while knowing that you need others around you. The thing about a desire for freedom to live life to the full is that you have to abide by some degree of rules and restrictions – no matter how much you try and resist.

Six-year-old Max's parents, John and Karen, were already juggling a busy lifestyle, looking after their son and his two-year-old sister, Martha. Max has an undiagnosed genetic disorder that has left him non-verbal and unable to do anything for himself. He has complex epilepsy with different kinds of seizures every day.

In 2019 the family started getting support from Children's Hospice at Home and have used various services they offer. Karen said, *'We heard about the Hospice at Home service when Max started at a special school, and Martha was just over one year old. They started helping us, and it was just great having somebody who could sit with Max after school and understand Max's needs or what to do if he had a seizure while I was picking up Martha from the nursery. It meant that I didn't have to move him around or get him in and out of the car, which was really useful'.* She explains, *'It's great to know that you have 24-hour support and someone you can talk to. Even if they don't have the answer, someone is there to discuss it with you, and that's so comforting. Especially if you get to the weekend and know he's not great, it's good to know they're there. It's quite a small team, and they have regular meetings, so even if we haven't met that particular member of staff, you feel that they know him. Sometimes there's a lot of pressure on us as parents to make these judgement calls, and it's nice to share it with somebody else, which we've done at other times'.*

Alongside the Hospice at Home service and support from organisations like Supporting Hands Volunteer Service, the family has attended many events organised by The Pepper Foundation and Children's Hospice. Here they can talk to other families and build up an extended network of people who want to support each other and know exactly what it is like to love and care for a member of the family who depends on ongoing support. Karen made the point that it is nice not having to explain what it is like all of the time and just feeling like you belong.

Do you remember, in chapter one, I described the various versions of the question 'why' I received when I explained what I was going to attempt? The excited smiles that awakened a long-dormant childlike sense of adventure in the listener. And the sarcastic version that displayed a total lack of life perspective (in my humble opinion, at least). And, of course, there were the stunned silences and sideways looks at Penny. I often feel like people's reactions to disability fall into similar categories. Surely, getting involved in other people's lives, fears, hopes and dreams (only when invited, of course) is the best way to approach any other person, regardless of their situation. Let's not even ask *why* in such cases. It's about finding out what we can do to help and offering our services and resources as part of the solution.

I met lots of people as I cycled, ran, swam and kayaked my way around the country. Some asked why; some shared their stories with me and taught me great lessons, others were old friends who came to support my journey, and there were a few who gave me precious moments I will treasure for the rest of my life. When I think of children like Max, and his parents, I remember how important it is to value what you have each day and be grateful for the people we have in our lives: both those we know and the kindness of strangers. I am in awe of families like this because their love drives them on regardless of circumstance and their example positively affects others. And therein lies the most important thing I learned from Max's story. While the family were grateful for the support and friendship they received from various charities and healthcare services, they were unaware that they inspired and encouraged others in return. Their strength and fortitude would have been as positively and vibrantly contagious at those social events as the joy they found in talking to others in similar circumstances. Love and support are more powerful than any virus, and *that* is the pandemic we should be eager to spread.

Love and care can adapt to any situation

As the implications of the COVID-19 pandemic became part of everyone's consciousness and reality in March 2020, another new word entered John and Karen's vocabulary. They were forced to consider the idea of shielding a six-year-old boy who already suffered from daily seizures, vomiting and susceptibility to other health issues. They had to adapt very quickly and carefully to ensure his safety. So while most still had *some* contact with the outside world, even during the strictest periods of lockdown, Max's family could not afford to take that risk. And yet their son needed support - and lots of it.

John began working from home, Karen was furloughed (which gave her time to look after the children), and Martha was kept home from nursery to help keep Max safe. Karen said, *'Max has seizures every day and several types of different seizures. He just needs everything doing for him; he can't do any activities on his own, so like with our home-schooling, most of the time, it's just me trying to do things for both of them. Martha, she's only two, but she likes to do things to help him'.*

24-hour phone support became the main lifeline to the outside world. Karen believes this support has been priceless and recalls, *'The nurses regularly phoned to make sure we didn't need anything and helped with Max's recent medication change and taking care of things. This has meant that we've been able to stay at home, which is what we've wanted'.* However, there was little else they could do for most of the seventeen months of national lockdown in the UK because even as the regulations eased, the shielding element meant minimum contact was allowed. One concern Karen told us had played on her mind continuously, adding to the pressure, was, *'If we had both got so ill that we couldn't care for him or had to isolate completely, we would have been really stuck. Even if it had been just one of us, the other would have to deal with both of them on their own, which is really hard. It made us think: we don't have a backup plan. We have no one else who can care for him, so it was a big worry'.*

As I write this chapter of the book (August 2021), services at the Hospice are beginning to resume (along with various other support services). The family is looking forward to working with their specialist nurses to find safe ways to interact again. This will also allow Martha to return to nursery and see all her friends again. Karen said, *'We feel that organisations like the Children's Hospice will help us get back to normality as a lot of what they do is about quality of life, and that's why all the activities we do with them are so wonderful. Sometimes the Children's Hospice supports us to go on trips and try new places. Having someone else there makes all the difference – you wouldn't want to spend all that money, and it then is a disaster, which happens! So, it really is about quality of life with a child as complex as Max as we don't know what's around the corner'.* The couple has shared how the involvement of the Children's Hospice nurses has impacted Max's and the whole family's lives and, although lockdown has been testing, John added, *'It's not particularly one thing; it's all of it. The knowledge that the support base is still there has made a massive difference'.*

As we return to my adventures in the following chapters, I would encourage you to remember Aayushi and Max and their families, and perhaps just as importantly, the people who work for and volunteer at the services that support them. If you would like to offer support to these organisations, the details are throughout this book, and that help would be greatly appreciated. But I would also like you to consider two other things. Do you appreciate the freedoms you have in your life, and do you appreciate the people around you who actively contribute to the life you have?

CHAPTER NINE

ALL ALONE AND EVERYTHING AGAINST YOU

After seven days of gruelling effort, combined with the emotional highs and lows of the unexpected and the poorly planned, I was glad to reach day eight, my first rest day. It came at the perfect time because, although I didn't know it then, the pressure of being alone for the entirety of the following day would be even more challenging.

While my body was grateful for the rest, and I thoroughly enjoyed the reassuring company of family and friends who had come up to West Kirby for the day, my mind was still partially on the day ahead. However, I found some comfort from the knowledge that the challenge had been frontloaded in terms of physical difficulty. So, even though I was only a quarter of the way in, I was now 100% sure of my ability to complete the course. It was reassuring.

Getting the hard stuff out of the way early on has always served me well in life and usually paves the way for a more positive and confident finish. I have found that to be a great way to approach any hurdle. If you attack the scariest or most unpleasant part of the task first, it puts you in the mindset of knowing the day or week should always get easier from there on in. In practical terms, that is not always the way life deals our cards, of course. But your mindset is critical and means you are best placed to handle whatever comes next.

I think that is what I like most about the stories I just shared. Many people struggled with the lockdown period, physically and emotionally, but these families were already well-versed in dealing with extraordinary circumstances and doing whatever was necessary out of love. So for them, it was just a case of turning up the resilience and going again. What a lot there is to learn from other people's stories if only we would listen.

The big boost to your energy is seeing those you love!

So... I thoroughly enjoyed the physical rest, and it was made all the more special by spending it with Penny and the children. Of course, I enjoyed telling Penny how sensible I had been by choosing to avoid the Severn crossing, even if the disappointment was still ringing constantly around in my mind like a faulty car alarm. And she, in turn, shared some news from home. The children were just happy to see their dad, and likewise, it was great to be with them all again.

My good friends, Anne and Mark Consedine and their son Ned, came up for the day too, and it was good to share more details of the journey so far with such positive supporters of our endeavours. Anne, in particular, had been responsible for a lot of the fabulous PR we had generated for the challenge, as well as helping with the planning. It was a very relaxing day which, as a result of the people around me, turned into a mini-celebration of the story so far. But there was still a bit of work to do, and a part of my mind was never far from the anticipation of tomorrow. Between talking, laughing and enjoying the company of friends, having a well-earned massage and carrying out a bit of bike maintenance, there was some re-planning that needed my attention.

**Sadly, Anne passed away suddenly from cancer only a few years later. The news rocked our family, but we have been so impressed and inspired by how Mark and Ned dealt with such a tragic loss. They are incredible examples of how people can cope through the very worst of times with the love and support of family and friends. Anne's legacy is another great example of truly valuing the time we have on this earth.*

Even in rest, your mind can play a major role in working smarter

We live in the centre of the information age. Never before has there been a time that the average human mind has been bombarded with more information per minute than it is today. And when you are surrounded by that environment (in the average office and home), your brain rarely has a chance to stop and truly unwind. That is why it is essential to have time off, holidays, rest days, tech-free days, outdoor days and a healthy conversational homelife. However, even when you get those elements right, a tiny piece of your mind is always working on something in the background.

My theory is that the more time you spend in a 'busyness-free' environment, the more that magical part of your brain is allowed to do its mysterious and wonderful work. Even if it is just giving it the awareness to spot opportunities, the clear-mindedness to solve long-lasting problems, or the distance to see the bigger picture with more clarity, your time off can be super-valuable.

Hindsight is only as valuable as what you learn from it, and I learned a lot that I would do differently if I tried this trip again. I've said before that I was absolutely meticulous in my eighteen months of planning before the event, but nothing was ever going to be quite like the real thing. In those first seven days, I also learned a huge amount about myself, my equipment, the transitions, managing a support team, timing, distance, and the environment. It was experience and data that would serve me well for the rest of the challenge, and today (my rest day) was the perfect opportunity to build some of this information into the plan for the days to come. So I did!

That was not to say that there wouldn't still be difficulties ahead. I knew that not every day was going to turn out as perfect as yesterday had been and that a plan was needed, so I had a basis from which to adjust. It was lovely to see my friends and family again, but, as usual, that made it all the harder to say goodbye and focus on turning tomorrow's plan into action. Simon was also leaving that day and the thought of facing the next few days on the road alone was a step into the unknown. I suppose that was somewhat like Aayushi and Max's parents must have felt as lockdown descended in March 2020.

When it feels like everything is against you

The ominous sub-title to introduce day nine describes exactly how I felt. It had been good to have a rest the day before because the first week had been seriously challenging physically. But exhaustion was easy to deal with. The next few days held a different challenge – they would be emotionally tough.

Tony, my faithful driver and right-hand man, would still be meeting me at the transition points, of course, but this was the first day where I would take on every step, peddle, paddle and stroke by myself. I said goodbye to Penny and the children again that morning, knowing it would be twelve days before I saw them again. Even with my renewed plan in hand and the confidence that I could overcome the physical challenge, the reality of heading out on the bike that morning weighed far more than I had anticipated.

As I said earlier, mindset is the key aspect of any test, and it can be especially helpful if you can set it before the pressure sets in. Trying to recapture the right attitude while allowing a negative one to run riot in your head is like trying to fix a puncture without getting off the bike. I still don't fully understand how I managed to get myself in that state, but the self-talk in my head that morning was consuming. And add to the loneliness of each mile the fact that the route itself was largely uncharted territory, I really was starting to feel the pressure. My previous record for an endurance event had only lasted nine days, so I was also beginning to question my body and stamina in areas that hadn't been broached before. Considering my earlier statement about confidence in the ability to make it all the way, that meant I was effectively back-pedalling.

Sometimes, the toughest tests are not actually the toughest situations we have to face in life. More often than not, there is a shoulder to cry on, a wise old head to give you advice or an expert to refer to when facing an uphill stretch. If there is a lesson to learn from my feelings, even before this day had got going, it is that whenever you possibly can, make sure a helping hand is at your side.

I don't necessarily want to use up too many words of this book on COVID-19 – we all want to move on as best we can. Each of us will have different memories, some more devastating than others. But one thing I'm confident most of us now share is a new appreciation of humankind. Of neighbours showing they care. Of friends getting back in touch. Of families distanced by miles making an effort to get and stay connected, despite the miles between them. Communication has become the new buzzword. The Baby Boomer generation has merged with Generations X, Y and Z to embrace technology amid the limitations of self-isolation and social distancing.

I believe that social media is possibly one of the best communication tools ever developed, and now, especially, that's proven to be so. And yet, it's also a double-edged sword as it can be far from social for some. Let me explain. Throughout the pandemic, we saw a seismic shift in the levels of communication and awareness between neighbours, friends and family. In some ways, (bear with me!) isolation could be compared to losing one of our five senses, like hearing or sight. The others become heightened. We couldn't meet up, so we found other ways to connect: messaging, social media platforms, video calls.

It's possible that, before the pandemic, friends thought social media platforms gave all the insight necessary to understand, or even be aware of, any sadness or troubles we were going through. They were 'up to speed' with your life, so they didn't need to pick up the phone or meet up. There's no fault or finger-pointing intended here. It's a twenty-first-century affliction. When reading the post on a friend's 'wall', it's too easy to assume they are telling the true story of their lives. But not many of us do tell the truth in that way. We paint the picture we want others to see - we put on our game face and pretend all is well. We try not to burden others.

But...when we pick up the phone and talk or invite them to a video call, we can hear the hidden messages in their words and see the sadness in their eyes if it's there. And we can be there for them. The pandemic has hopefully changed the way we communicate and use social media. We may start to be more honest and more aware of others. We may continue what we've begun in such difficult times;

appreciating and celebrating friendships. Inflate more balloons, even! I know I'm going to. And I'm thankful for every day on my bonkers journey around the UK that my equally bonkers friends, and those not quite so bonkers, made an effort to support me through actual visits, phone calls and messages.

Fight your way through to the familiar

Back to my *'dies horriblis'*...The day began with a bike ride from West Kirby, where I had spent the rest day, heading for Fort Perch Rock at the mouth of Liverpool's Mersey River. Poor weather and the fact that I was fighting off feelings of insecurity and self-pity meant I erred on the side of caution again and decided not to attempt the crossing. On another day, with a braver, more positive mindset, I think I might have attacked it and had I done so, I believe the victory would have restored my faith. I have discovered that yesterday's regrets have little value in today's actions, but letting a little of the 'what if' linger can drive you forward the next time. So, after missing out on that part of the adventure, it was back on the bike at Crosby and a long, solitary bike ride up through Preston and head-down, feet to the pedals, pressing on to Lancaster.

The weather was dull, wet, misty and foreboding, reflecting my mood and doing its best to dampen it further. As the hours piled on and I was left alone with my thoughts and a lifeless landscape, I approached the potentially picturesque City of Lancaster. I had been looking forward to seeing it again, and it was a part of the route that had appealed to me in the planning. I'm not a superstitious person, nor do I believe in good or bad luck, but it does seem to be the case that when you set your mind in one position, you tend to see a reflection. As I approached the place, I recalled my earlier expectations, and it seemed (to me at least) that the sun showed a little sympathy in response to my heightened anticipation and made a bit of an appearance. And by the time I reached the Lake District and prepared myself for the climbs to come, the entire outlook had changed.

I love Cumbria, and arriving among its peaks and lakes certainly lifted my spirits to another level. There were six tough climbs to face when I arrived, and I could not have been more excited by the challenge.

It was as though a different Richard to the one who left Crosby that morning had arrived in the afternoon: ready to take on as much as there was in front of him. Beyond those wonderfully challenging climbs on the bike was a short swim and a delightful run that brought me to a well-earned rest in Gosforth. So the day of doom ended on an incredible high (albeit a tired one) that I could not have even imagined a few hours earlier. Isn't life funny like that? It's another reason I believe in the power of positive thought. *"There is a solution to every problem; the trick is to find the solution before you encounter the consequence",* Robert Vondersaar.

Being an adventurous person, I live for the highs; I revel in the challenges, and I get the biggest buzz of all from coming out of the other side of adversity. If you look back on your life experiences, you will probably see the same pattern of highs and lows, recurring scenarios and emotions. We all love life when we are winning. For example, our application for a mortgage is accepted, and we can live in the house of our dreams. Maybe when our favourite team wins the cup or we are offered a promotion at work. And especially when a baby is born or a big birthday is celebrated. Equally, we revel in the end of a problem; when we get the all-clear from the doctor, a dreaded event sorts itself out, or something valuable, thought lost forever, is found.

My point is that, as long as we can always look out for the proverbial *'light at the end of the tunnel'* or imagine a bright horizon to aim for, we can pretty much get through anything. The key is to deal with the reality in front of you. Keep your head down and keep the pedals moving, but ensure your mind is set on the right things while you put in the effort. Physical challenges are easy if you are prepared and working at your level (or just above, to keep it interesting!). The real battle is always emotional (especially loneliness). But you can get through loneliness by remembering it is temporary. At some point, as most of us were fortunate to witness throughout the more challenging days of the pandemic, you will speak to, hear from, and see someone that matters. And when you have sorted out the self-talk and overthinking going on in your head, focus on the future: keep peddling until you get where you're going. What other choice do you have?

I suppose my thoughts on that day could be summed up in a line from my favourite poem: If, by Rudyard Kipling. In the second verse, he writes:

'If you can meet with Triumph and Disaster,
and treat those two impostors just the same.'

For me, that means everything. I would encourage you to go and look up the entire poem – it's wonderful.

Maybe inspired by Kipling, or just my inbuilt stubbornness, I choose to keep going. And my reward during the rest of my journey included storms, seals, magical bridges, ancient forests, mountain peaks, dangerous descents, Tolkienish travels, storming a castle and chariots of fire. What adventures might lay ahead for you if you keep your head up and keep peddling?

DAY 9

Liverpool

Entering Lake District

CHAPTER TEN

HOW SCOTLAND CHANGED THE LANDSCAPE OF MY LIFE

You know that experience where you haven't seen a niece, nephew or a close friend's younger children for several years and, when you do see them, you notice the small but significant changes? Compare that to when you see older friends and relatives. The difference is never quite as dramatic, is it? Unless, of course, they have lost weight, changed hair colour, or gone under the knife!

When you comment to the child about how you can see changes, it can be annoying to them. We all know that because we remember it from our own childhood. But, as you look at them and note the height, looks or maturity in their manner, there is no question of the change taking place. The thing is, those close to them barely noticed those changes. They spend each day together while the transformation passes by under their noses.

Life events can be the same for people. Perhaps you survived a health concern, spent the last two years studying in the evenings to pass an exam or have been dealing with the loss of a loved one for some time. How we cope with these episodes in our lives shapes us (for better or worse). It determines the person who travels into future days on our behalf. As adults, we often think that we are who we have become, and we will remain this way for the rest of our lives. But the fact is that obstacles, victories, bad luck and good fortune will continue to shape our personality and the way we deal with things for as long as we live.

There are two things I want to highlight at this point. Firstly, you can control some of the things that make you a better person by deliberately challenging and pushing yourself beyond what you think is possible. And secondly, it is crucial to stop, take stock, and look back at where you have changed from time to time. Otherwise, like the teenager who wanders from kitchen to bedroom around your house, you might miss some of the most important days of your life.

So, in this chapter, I want to compare the person who entered Scotland, on day ten of my journey, with the one who exited its bonnie shores on day twenty (older, wiser and a whole lot thinner). You may ask what can have changed in ten days, but that is just my point. If you embark on an adventure with purpose, you can measure growth and resilience in days, not years. And after finishing on day twenty, I'll describe the experiences that brought about the change.

New-determination, near-death experiences and nicer days ahead!

If I thought the conditions had been challenging (mentally, physically and emotionally), as I made my way up the northwest coast of England, I'd underestimated the resolve of their intent. Tired from the ascents and descents of yesterday's Cumbrian quest, I set off from Gosforth with renewed vigour but was met with equal defiance from the elements lying in wait to greet me – namely Scotland! But I was ready. At least, I thought I was...

Not so 'bonnie' Scotland and a brush with fear

A bracing 60km on the bike, with lots more climbing, brought me to Skinburness on the English coast of the Solway Firth, where I received a chilling welcome to our Celtic neighbours' lands. This kayak was another of those *'marginal'* decisions, but I was determined not to turn back this time. Had I made different calls on the previous two crossings, I might have turned away from this one, but I had to show the wind and the rain that I meant business and where better than on these ancient northern waterways. It was perhaps lousy timing for a renewal of my belligerent determination because the wind-driven advancing tide, hiding its numerous sandbanks just below the surface, was busily mixing up high waves and choppy conditions. Not ideal for kayaking!

The crossing was 15km in total, the longest of the whole adventure, and at every stroke, I was hounded and harassed by side-on white-water attacks. I even experienced a rare moment of genuine apprehension which quickly manifested into fear – a completely new experience for me. Turning back was no longer an option as I was already more than halfway across but looking forward was horrifying. I had capsized earlier in the trip, landing on the beach in Cornwall, but that had been only a few meters from the shore – not several kilometres – this was very different, and it was serious. Fear starts in your eyes. As you take stock of the situation, it then quickly moves to your heart, where automated, uncontrollable panic messages are sent to every inch of your body. You can almost feel the hyper-energy moving through your limbs. And while this may be a natural reaction designed by the body to keep us alive in the face of life-threatening situations, it is not actually what we need. The best course of action when you are in genuine danger and facing the very real prospect of drowning (or any emergency) is to keep calm and concentrate on what matters. For me, at that moment in time, I could not afford for the adrenaline to tense my muscles, the panic to make me thrash wildly at the waves, or for my exhaustion to take over. I had to focus on staying upright as each subsequent wave smashed into the kayak, and white-water stallions leapt from the water all around me. I had trained for moments like this, learned the subtle skill of using my paddle to balance and spent hours in my kayak becoming familiar with its reactions to the waves – I could do this if I concentrated.

Eventually (I am not quite sure how), I made it across, mentally and physically spent, and just collapsed for a while as my heart slowly regained its senses and convinced the rest of my body everything would be OK. I had been in one or two tense situations before, but I can't think of any scenario where I was quite that scared. It was not an emotion I expected nor one I am used to experiencing. So (perhaps for all the wrong reasons – and only in retrospect) I relished its appearance.

It all comes back to 'why?'

I said in an earlier chapter that when I spoke to people about my experiences on this journey, during the build-up and even before reaching the starting line, they usually asked 'why?'. I always explained that there are many answers to this question, and the ones I gave depended mainly on the tone in which the 'why' was asked.

There is the charity angle and wanting to give something back; also, the opportunity to see so many wonderful places and do things most people rarely get to do. But, if I'm honest (and I always try to be), most of it comes down to my need to satisfy a hunger within! I don't really know how to explain it, and I believe that only those who share something similar can truly understand it, but I just need to know how far I can go – to get a handle on my limits. This crossing took me close to that point.

Will Smith once said (I'm paraphrasing), *"You might have more talent than me, be smarter than me, be sexier than me... you might be better in all categories than me. But if we get on the treadmill together, there's two things that are certain: you're getting off first, or I'm going to die. It's really that simple"*. And that sums up my attitude to any challenge I ever face (except the ones where a promise to Penny overrules it).

Across the other side, as I emerged from the waters and trudged through the last 20 metres of mud while dragging my kayak behind me, my mood was at a new low, and any humour I had left was poor. Tony had been talking to some onlookers who had gathered on the far side to welcome me back to wet land. I'm ashamed to say I was a degree less than civil to them as I emerged... If they are reading this now, I'm offering a genuine, heartfelt – *"Sorry!"*

My last glance back as I left the Solway Firth behind me revealed a sign saying: *Danger. Strong currents, hidden channels, swimming not advised.* Not the first nor the last time I had seen a sign too late. I would probably have ignored it anyway.

Welcome to the west coast of Scotland

I had expected to finish the crossing in around an hour and a half, so the three hours plus that it actually took put a few time pressures on the rest of the day. Despite all of that, it was good to set foot on Scottish soil and know that I had reached that milestone at last: another little victory and a decisive step towards my bigger goal. Despite its harsh initial greeting, my reward for still loving Scotland was being surrounded by stunning countryside for the subsequent cycle, swim and run, which completed day ten. And it even brightened up a little later in the afternoon.

If I had known what was in store for the rest of my travels in Scotland, I'm sure the anticipation would have rendered me too excited to sleep. Who could even imagine such a journey if not sandwiched between a Hollywood movie's opening and closing credits?

The most understated, most memorable border-crossing of my life

As I mentioned earlier, I will let the following three or four chapters explain what happened to change things for me, but I want to skip ahead a little for the rest of this one and reveal a little about how I emerged from Scotland.

Day twenty (my final morning in Scotland) began with a long cycle ride. This one was some 102km, and I was on a mission because we had arranged lunch with some of my relatives just North of Berwick-upon-Tweed. It was lovely to stop and catch up with friendly faces, but the pressure was on to keep going and move on to Holy Island.

An unscheduled detour had taken me inland the previous day, so my route had been a slightly different one from what I would have taken. But that circumstance meant I chanced upon one of the quaintest little bridges I have ever seen, beckoning me over the River Tweed and back to England's green and pleasant shores. The Union Bridge at Horncliffe is a unique little chain bridge and is the oldest suspension bridge in the UK. The selfie I took there is one of my favourites from the entire four weeks. It is special for several reasons: the fact that it is a quirky, picturesque bridge that few people, outside of the locals, ever get to see, and because it did mark the crossing of a national border.

As I re-entered England and waved goodbye to ten memory-packed days of hard graft, magical scenes, friendly people, the harshest and kindest of weather and the fresh, cool air of the country's northerly lands, I took a moment to consider. Scotland had challenged me. It had smiled at me, taken my breath away at times, but always had the good grace to give it back at the end of each day. Thank you, Scotland.

From the bridge at Horncliffe, I cycled back to the coast and across the causeway to Holy Island, and what a ride that was. With no land obstructions and the wind right behind me, I reached a speed of 48km per hour on the bike across the causeway, my fastest 'on the flat' stretch of the whole adventure (where is a speed camera when you need one). Holy Island is aptly named and, despite the hoards of tourists that visit throughout the year and could be seen in abundance that day, it definitely gives off an innate serenity and beauty, which made it a highlight of the east coast.

From Holy Island, Tim (Mayes) and I got into the kayak (I had finally persuaded him to join me), and we paddled past Lindisfarne Castle, around the headland and down to Bamburgh Castle. We were, once again, joined by a bob of curious seals bobbing up and down around us. Incidentally, I looked this up and thought it worth sharing, just in case you are interested too. There are several collective nouns for a group of seals: a colony, a rookery, a herd, a harem, but my favourite is the one I've used: a bob of seals. It so aptly describes what you see when you encounter this wondrous creature amongst its many friends and family. On the day they allowed us to join them, they were clearly enjoying the ocean's glorious sunshine and deep blueness as much as we were. It was utterly joyful to be part of it.

The day finished with a cycle ride, taking the team and me down to Creswell and a well-earned good night's sleep in the campervan.

The battle of east and west and north and south

As I drifted off to sleep that night, I couldn't help but compare the crossing of England into Scotland ten days earlier with what I had done this day. In one instance, I was seemingly fighting for my life against the harshest winds, waves and tides of the west and, in the other, enjoying a gentle, sunshiny freewheel over a quaint little wooden bridge. I think the smile on my face as I approached dreamland that night was not actually the contrast at all: it was the self-revealing realisation that I probably enjoyed the first crossing the most. Most of all, I realised that ten days in Scotland had changed my perspective.

Any adventure is full of its ups and downs, with victories and challenges along the way. But wouldn't you agree that it's often the bigger picture that sees you through in the end? And there is rarely any doubt that any lessons you take from it will make you stronger for the next time. It seems appropriate to quote another few lines from Rudyard Kipling here:

'If you can force your heart and nerve and sinew
To serve your turn long after they are gone,
And so hold on when there is nothing in you
Except the Will which says to them: 'Hold on!'

DAY 12

Scotland England border Horncliffe Bridge

Union Bridge

Arisaig

CHAPTER ELEVEN

SOMETIMES TAKING PART *IS* ABOUT WINNING

I doubt many reading this book will disagree with me when I say: making commitments and creating deadlines helps us remain focused and achieve our goals. I'm taking you back to day eleven of my itinerary, which was always meant to be a big effort day with a deadline; we planned it that way. We knew it would either A) Provide a good jump-start if previous days hadn't gone according to plan, giving us the safety net to get us back on track should we need it. Or B) If we made good time and got ahead of ourselves, we could get a welcome 'bonus' rest just over one-third of the way into the challenge. Whichever outcome we achieved would be a victory, and I firmly believe that we should all celebrate and enjoy victories. Who cares what anyone else thinks?

Deadlines, good times and drawing attention to myself!

I had 136km to travel on the bike to get to Inverkip and unload the kayak so Tony could get on the 1pm ferry from a little further up the road at McInroy's Point. So setting off at two minutes to six, I started one of the longest cycles of the whole endeavour. It was not a particularly hard route, beautiful and still with its fair share of climbs (this was Scotland after all), but relatively uneventful. And while every day of the challenge was governed mainly by time, for this particular leg, it was critical. Missing that ferry would put everything out by hours and have a negative knock-on effect for days.

In hindsight, I probably shouldn't have agreed to be interviewed by the local paper in the midst of one of the most time-sensitive sections of the entire route...but I had. At least the short detour to answer a few questions with the Ardrossan and Saltcoats Herald reporter and pose for a picture gave me time to catch my breath. Despite the journalistic interlude, I arrived in good time just over seven hours after setting off (averaging around 21km per hour). After a smooth transition, Tony was on his way, and I hit the water once more.

Target achieved and plain sailing ahead

Compared to the day before, this was a lovely experience. As I entered the Firth of Clyde in the kayak, having enjoyed my bacon sandwich and an easy stroll down to the water's edge, I was feeling completely content. I was on time, felt unhurried, unburdened and even able to make a few phone calls from the kayak while giving way to a larger vessel – a tanker that was speeding along the Firth of Clyde.

There is nothing that sets you up for a good day or a strong performance quite like coming off the back of hitting a deadline. This was very much the case here, and it was helped by the fact that the sun was shining its peace upon the crossing. Often in life, we can be daunted by the enormity of a challenge or a task ahead of us: perhaps it is a time-critical one, or maybe a tough ask that simply has to get done. One of the secrets to motivating yourself through those mammoth efforts is dwelling on the knowledge that the victory will taste sweet and the 'future you' will appreciate your effort.

Smiling to myself and enjoying the sights and sounds of that particular kayak crossing, you might think I afforded myself a little pat on the back for having reached my target in plenty of time. I didn't. Maybe this is a weakness of mine (among many, I'm sure) but I usually want to move on to the next challenge with minimum fuss and attention. I talk a little more about this at the end of the adventure when (spoiler alert) I finally arrive back in Bournemouth to accolades I didn't really want. I like to treat success and failure as two sides of the same coin; I find that is the best way to get through both emotions. I know not everyone will agree with me on that point, so here is another angle you might prefer. Genuine self-validation is not boastfulness. It's acknowledging that you have done something well and are pleased with the result. Self-validation and taking time to realise your successes is good for self-esteem, and anything that contributes to well-balanced self-esteem *must* be good for our wellbeing. So perhaps, on reflection, I will work on that a little harder in the future.

How to draw a crowd and make them think

After the kayak crossing, another 35km on the bike brought me to Inverary, where we had planned to stop for the night. The campsite here was stunning, and I couldn't resist having an extra swim after my short run. I was even able to draw a small, curious crowd as people gathered on the balcony of the campsite's visitor centre overlooking Loch Fyne.

As I looked up from the water, watching them watching me, I couldn't help imagining what they might be thinking. Perhaps, "Why is that crazy man swimming in that freezing snow and ice fed water, seemingly going nowhere?" If only they knew the entire extent of the crazy enterprise I was endeavouring to complete! It did make me smile to myself and wonder, could being famous be fun after all? In truth, I have no desire to find out, nor did I believe I was famous, of course – not for one moment. It was just a very welcome sight to see I wasn't alone, that people were taking an interest, and that they might find it in their hearts to donate to The Pepper Foundation.

The aggressive beauty of the Highlands, bathed in gentle sunshine, is undoubtedly one of the world's most remarkable sights. In fact, my whole time in Scotland was a mixture of those extremes: wind-dominated, angry storms and driving rain or dramatic, stunning landscapes blessed by blue skies and touched by the sun. This morning was a mixture of both.

The unexpected lurks around the corner, and he's feeling mischievous!

It was an idyllic start to the day on the bike. Setting out early, I completed 86km of joyfully beautiful scenery, ending in one of the most picturesque parking areas I've ever seen: and all before breakfast! As I arrived in Cuil Bay, ready for some bacon and eggs, my heart warmed to the cool blue, flat and still waters awaiting my kayak across the bay.

It was so millpond-still that as I tucked into that morning's fuel, I almost felt guilty that I would be the one to disturb its surface. It was a bit like the mixed feelings you have (both childlike joy and destructive shame) at walking through freshly fallen snow.

You'd have thought I'd learned all about the laws of unpredictability by now, but half an hour later, by the time I entered the water, the wind had descended, and it started to erupt. Isn't it true in life, occasionally, what begins as a calm event can turn into what seems like a maelstrom without warning? Surely we should all know: that's life! Prepare for the unexpected. In reality, many of us don't always remember to do so and to be fair, sometimes no amount of preparation will change a situation. Like the one that descended on me that day.

This particular maelstrom didn't deter me, however. The fact that it was unexpected made it even more appealing in many ways, and the reward of seeing Ben Nevis ascend towards the skyline over to the right made it all the more special. So if I can offer any advice, it is this: yes, try and be as prepared as you can. But if you can't, enjoy the thrill of being uncomfortable. Enjoy the rewards you'll get for an achievement.

To add to the joy of a tumultuous crossing, I shared the water with a family of seals who bobbed and weaved around me as I bounced from wave to wave.

No room for a fall in a boggy fell run

After the kayak across the bay, all 13km of it, I hit the road for 40km on the bike before arriving at another unexpected obstacle. This one took me by surprise because the map makers clearly hadn't visited for some time. Why would they? It wasn't the sort of place normal people go very often, although I think prehistoric cave dwellers would have felt very much at home.

I was looking for the footpath the map had promised me would be there to guide my run up the steep fell and over the other side to my awaiting swim. It was about 5km, and most of that was pathless boggy mud, occasionally up to my knees. However, I have to say; it was excitingly fabulous, exotically ancient, mysteriously magical, and left you with the feeling you were very far from anywhere, in both distance and time. I loved it!

Being totally alone added to the thrill of that run (trudge), with no radio signal and no way of getting a message to anyone else if I fell or twisted an ankle. The danger and the thrill of needing to be extra careful with every step were exhilarating as I slowly and carefully made my way down the other side of the hill. Later Tony told me he had seen my orange bag momentarily emerge through the greenery before its grasp once more swallowed it up.

The joys of an ice bath

Although an ice bath at the end of each day is a favourite of many endurance athletes, it's not typically part of my routine, and I prefer the occasional cold shower to get me going in the mornings. However, I was unexpectedly and abruptly introduced to the bath variety on this day. Whether it was the fact the water's origin was the surrounding snow-capped mountains or just the nature of the Scottish air, I don't know, but the swim that followed was seriously cold. It was enough to take your breath away, hiding it at arm's length for a minute before reluctantly offering it back. It was far too cold even to become accustomed to after a few minutes and enough to spur on even the hardiest of adventurers to the other side – fast. In all seriousness, if you do ever find yourself swimming in icy water like I did that morning, the key is to go as fast as you can. That was a race to the other side with the genuine threat of hypothermia in pursuit—another thrilling memory.

What a fabulous day!

The obvious lesson to glean from day twelve is to expect the unexpected. But it is actually so much more than that. I have found that a better approach is to anticipate and totally embrace the unexpected! Not all surprises are good ones, but they mostly represent excitement, adventure, opportunity and learning: good or bad. The attitude with which you face everything (planned or unplanned) determines the result you achieve on the other side.

Looking at the bigger picture, I think that day was one of my favourites, and some elements are certainly on the revisit list.

 DAY 13

Loch Linnhe

Acharacle - Boggy run

Arisaig Sunset

CHAPTER TWELVE

YOU JUST HAD TO BE THERE!

I sincerely hope you are enjoying my recollections of 28 days of challenge and memory-making. But reading this book will never match getting out and living for yourself. Go on, give it a try! You'll be surprised at the mental and physical stamina and the resilience you can draw on when inspired to take on a challenge, especially if one of your goals is to raise money for a worthy cause (although that isn't a prerequisite, it's your choice). You will also, I promise, be astounded at the support you will receive from family, friends and well-wishers. I know I was.

Disappointment, discovery and ultimate delight

One of the (not wholly unexpected, but highly disappointing all the same) lessons that had made its mark so far in my journey was that the best-laid plans often prove impossible to complete. Yes, there was always a backup route, and I still managed to include all four of my chosen disciplines pretty much every day: but the few *'failed to complete'* moments still irked me.

Day thirteen was another kayak crossing where I would have been fighting an immovable headwind. It wasn't so much the danger element of this one (although dodging tankers in a busy shipping lane against the wind isn't exactly a safe pastime), but more the time it would have taken to complete. I estimated it would have used up around five hours of travel time to cross the 9km ferry route from Mallaig to Armadale in Skye. That would have been over half the day's travel time dedicated to less than 5% of the distance. Sometimes you just have to make sensible sacrifices for the greater good, glean any lesson from the situation that you can, and then move on.

Moving upwards: to the Skye and beyond...

My first ever visit to the Isle of Skye was a lovely experience, and being able to cycle across the magnificent Skye Bridge back to the mainland was special. Through those mystical, story-filled lands, that memorable cycle brought me to Stromeferry, where I came face to face with yet another idyllic image. This part of the challenge was often too beautiful for words to describe. It would be so easy for me to say, *'you had to be there'* to avoid the impossible task of describing one of the most delightful places on my whole adventure. And just like making hard decisions about leaving out a leg of the journey, sometimes the easy option is the right one. You had to be there!

There is a reason so many songwriters, poets, storytellers and myth makers emanate from north of the Scottish borders. The inspiration they drew from, and still do, is all around. From the heather and bracken covered hills and peaks to the dark blue waters of the lochs, Scotland is the perfect example of pictures speaking louder than words. But I said I wouldn't describe it. So, my words of wisdom for this chapter, overriding any that follow in the next few paragraphs? Visit Scotland.

Back on track, and more ancient Scottish magic

Leaving that wonderful, awe-inspiring place behind and riding back to the mainland via the bridge, I pedalled on through more epically isolated countryside: often feeling like I was the only man on earth and enjoying the thought. The road eventually brought me a little way past Shieldag to a harbour where I decided to take an unscheduled swim. It was one thing to forgo my kayak that day and not be able to replace it, but there was no way that the swim I'd also missed earlier was going to suffer. The water was freezing, but it was just great to be back on track, even if it was an impromptu leg of the journey. As I emerged from the icy depths, I was faced with a steep climb through the thick undergrowth of an ancient wooded area that still rang with the echoes of a bygone age. It seemed that every time I went *'off piste'* and indulged in spontaneity, the magic of the Highlands descended and came alive. I was in my element again.

Catching up with Tony and the support vehicle at the top, I got back on the bike and set off to meet my good friend Mike Fairrie (all-round sportsman and watersports fanatic). It was only as I pushed through those last few lonely miles that it dawned on me how much I had missed the company: it was so good to see him!

Old friends, new friends and redemption

Meeting Mike in Gairloch was a game-changer for me at this point in the challenge. I'm not entirely sure why: maybe it's because I had got a bit carried away with the depths of my own thoughts and imaginations while battling each challenge alone the past few days. Or perhaps the prehistoric scenery and its ancient calling had distracted me from the task at hand. But as soon as Mike arrived, and I greeted him with the longest, most emotion-filled hug I have ever given another man in my life, my focus came back tenfold! The look on Mike's face at this unexpected show of affection said it all, and no words were needed.

Instead of lingering on the morning's disappointment, as I might have done if left to my own devices, but spurred on by Mike's presence, we immediately opted for a 5km kayak from Badachro across the bay to Gairloch – just because the water was there. Afterwards, we were treated to a delightful meal with Mike's cousins, Doug and Leila, to set us up for the second half of the adventure. Lovely place and lovely people.

A big cycle, a deep sleep, a mighty storm, then wallop!

Hitting the halfway mark (day fourteen) was supposed to be momentous. Having Mike with me was supposed to be the lift I needed to re-energise my efforts. Reaching the top of Scotland and heading east in the direction of John o'Groats was supposed to be one of the big landmarks of the entire endeavour. None of that happened. In fact, quite the opposite occurred. I was totally floored (almost literally), and the whole challenge very nearly came crashing down around me.

We set off on the bikes, business as usual and everything as planned. Or so we thought. The wind was once more against us, making it challenging from the outset, but I employed a determined head-down and go attitude, spurred on by having my cycling partner Mike alongside me. We were due to kayak early on, after 35km, but the winds were challenging enough on two wheels, so we opted to stay on the road instead and agreed we should hit the waves later in the day when we stopped for our planned swim and run.

We were 130km into a seriously tough, wind-opposed cycle ride across the most northern coastline of Scotland, and my body finally said 'no'. It wasn't a moaning, whiny 'no' but more of a definitive, stubborn refusal to carry on any longer. Mike had dropped some way behind me; I was freewheeling rapidly along a fairly lengthy descent, and... slowly... I simply drifted off to sleep. Obviously, I don't remember too much about it, although I *can* say it was a genuine first for me! Mike later described the gradual sidewinding motion as I veered to the right into the opposite lane. If you think the fact that there was no oncoming traffic to the right was lucky, consider the consequences of sleep-riding left and straight off the cliff edge! I imagine I would have hit the headlines for all the wrong reasons. (Although, don't they say that all publicity is good publicity?)

This was no marginal decision

Amazingly, despite having fallen asleep while riding my bike downhill on a narrow and winding Highland road, I did not fall off. As I left the road onto the grass verge, I woke with a start and managed to maintain my balance until I came to a shaky stop. By the time Mike had caught up, it was evident that I couldn't go any further.

As we had another 30km of road until we reached our campsite in Durness, and there was no choice but to try and get there. If there is one warning sign in my life that speaks even louder, clearer (and with more absolute authority than Penny), it is my body. This was no marginal decision – it was time to stop! So we climbed into the motorhome and let Tony drive us the last few kilometres. It was a tough decision, but the right one, and we eventually arrived at our destination. The run and swim for that day would have to be missed, but by that time, even I didn't care, I had to rest.

Incidentally, if you Google Friday the 17th of July 2015, you will read about the storms that wiped out the British Open at St Andrews, just across on the east coast from where we were at that stage of the challenge. The storm caused severe flooding and brought almost hurricane-level winds, causing devastating water and wind damage to the course and the entire area. So, on the night when I probably needed a refreshing five hours of sleep more than any other, I had the worst night of the whole challenge. The wind violently shook the motorhome the entire night, and all I could think about was the headline in the paper the next day telling how a kayak had killed campers as it was ripped from the roof and hurled around the campsite.

Looking for a port in the storm

Did this memorable (for all the wrong reasons) day teach me anything? Yes. It reminded me that the best-laid plans *can* get interrupted by stormy days. And it's one of the reasons The Pepper Foundation exists. When families hit unexpected turbulent waters after the news that a child has a life-threatening illness, they do the natural thing. They search for a port in that storm. They search for a lighthouse to guide them through those troubled waters. They look for an anchor point. Pepper provides all those things and more.

DAY 14

Highlands

CHAPTER THIRTEEN

A WELCOME REST IN PARADISE

Sango Sands sounds like it should be some kind of tropical paradise, doesn't it? Well, the people at the campsite were warm and generous; the restaurant was inviting and full of good food, and I'm sure that on a good day the views could be pretty spectacular (I'm told this is a great place to view the Northern Lights) but... paradise? Maybe not. However, it was undoubtedly a great sanctuary and the perfect place for me to rehab at a time when, oh boy, did I need a rest!

It was day fifteen, the second of my planned rest days and an excellent opportunity to take a bit of time out, gather my thoughts, recuperate, get a few supplies in and do a little preplanning for the days ahead. Having Mike with me added to the energy that I was able to generate during those precious hours of inactivity while my body enjoyed a few more hours of recovery mode. Could I find my winning mentality once more?

It takes more than legs to peddle!

When I say preplanning and gathering my thoughts, I really mean tweaking and reasserting myself to the task ahead. You see, the hard work of establishing a route, checking that there were places to cycle, swim, kayak and run, ensuring there were overnight locations and food stops, and finding enough friends to support my endeavours had already been done. The trip had been in the planning for around 18 months in all: the dream had been alive even longer still, and I had to remember that this 'time out' was all part of the bigger picture.

During the first half of the journey and the long hard miles that brought me to this point, I had been learning my trade. Nothing would actually be the same as doing the real thing, no matter what training I had done or plans and preparation I had put in place. That means I would need to continue learning, coping, adjusting and replanning all along the route, making sure each mile brought with it a better understanding of me, my equipment and the art of endurance.

Business is no different, and anyone going into an entrepreneurial venture would do well to take heed. You simply cannot get it right the first time. You can go to business school, earn diplomas, shadow a mentor, read books, study the experts and make the best business plan ever (in fact, you will *have* to do at least some of those things), but in the end, you still need to walk the walk.

The end of the mountains is in sight

So, as I sat in my pseudo paradise, enjoying the rest, thinking about the lessons of the last two weeks and pondering the challenges of the next two, I couldn't help but smile. It was not that there had ever been any *real* doubt in my mind that I would complete the course, despite the occasional wobble in my confidence (and the aforementioned incident on the bike!) but this day told me something significant. I had almost (but not quite) conquered the west coast of Scotland: by far the biggest, coldest and most formidable companion of my adventure. I had scaled its heights, swam in the cold depths of its lochs and lakes, tackled the roughest waves and strongest storms it could muster, and soaked up the fantastic views at every turn.

With the end of the mountains in sight, a good day's rest under my belt, and my good friend Mike ready to tackle the next day beside me, I slept well that night, looking forward to more promises of adventure in the second half of the Bonkers Challenge.

CHAPTER FOURTEEN

MEET RILEY, STANLEY AND SIENNA

Ask any fitness trainer, and they will tell you that rest is as important a factor in staying healthy as exercise. And if falling asleep on the bike reminded me of one thing, it was that we all have limits. But the thing about resting, recuperating and taking stock of your circumstances is: it gives you time to refocus and remember why you do the things you do and how fortunate you are. Being tired and overwhelmed by a situation is not the end of the road. It might mean you need to readjust, reevaluate or simply rest for a while but not that you are defeated. While there is a horizon to see, there is something of value worth fighting for.

So, in this chapter, we will meet some more of the incredible children and parents that The Pepper Foundation fund and support.

Riley and Stanley's story

Having a plan is always a good idea in life, whether you are circumnavigating Britain, saving up to buy a house or simply trying to get fit. But, whatever the size, extent or reason for your plan, the fact is you can only apply yourself to it one day at a time. Now, just imagine if your entire plan was to live one day at a time.

That is how brothers Riley and Stanley and their parents are forced to face life. Both boys were diagnosed at a young age with a very rare genetic condition involving duplication of an X-chromosome which has left them with very poor muscle tone and requiring constant care. They cannot sit, walk, talk or even feed properly, and the lack of knowledge about this condition means the specialists cannot predict what the future looks like for them.

The boys' parents, Shailza and Daniel, have bravely faced the situation, and their love for their sons has seen them through the first five years of the boys' lives. Thanks to the support of organisations like the Children's Hospice nurses and funding from The Pepper Foundation, they have moved into their own flat and can look after the boys at home most of the time. With ongoing support and the boys' constant smiles and giggles, Shailza and Daniel hope to see many more years together – always taking each day as it comes.

It is true to say that everyone reading this book will have suffered from the enforced lockdowns caused by the COVID-19 pandemic in 2020 and 2021, but for families who rely so heavily on support, it was particularly tough.

"The first lockdown coincided with Riley's muscle spasms becoming more frequent and intense," said Shailza. *"He was having really bad spasms that made him stiff, and they were happening so often that he was only getting about two and a half hours of sleep every 24 hours. He would doze off on my lap for about 20 minutes before another spasm woke him. It was awful to see him looking so ill. He was losing weight, exhausted and in pain."*

The entire family shielded during the first lockdown. Shailza explained, *"We were very cautious as we didn't know what we were dealing with or how it might affect the boys, especially Stanley, who has respiratory issues. But from September, we started having the nurses visit us again as I couldn't handle it anymore by myself"*.

At this point, Stanley was hospitalised for five days with a severe chest infection. *"He was so poorly,"* recalls Shailza, *"dehydrated and being sick constantly"*. That hospital stay was harder than usual because of COVID, and the risks and restrictions and uncertainty made everything more stressful.

It is hard to imagine what life must be like for families of children with severe disabilities and the children themselves who have only ever known that standard of life. And perhaps it is only when you come into contact with such strength, love, fortitude and dedication (both the families and those who support them) that you do stop and consider your own good fortune and life opportunities. I have not met Shailza and Daniel personally, I only heard about their story through The Pepper Foundation, but in my experience, people like this do not want your sympathy. They need your support, and any donations to the foundation are thankfully received. But I believe what they would also like you to take from their story is to be grateful.

I am happy to report that as the restrictions lifted, later in 2021, Riley and Stanley were both able to get back to school and carry on sharing their happiness and joy of life with their parents, nurses, teachers and anyone else who meets them.

As I enjoyed my rest, on day fifteen, I reflected on the previous two weeks, the fact that I was now halfway home and why I was in the middle of this crazy adventure. And the thought, as well as the rest, was what gave me the strength to get back on my legs, bike and kayak the following day.

Sienna's story

Now let's meet another courageous, resilient little girl.

At six years old, while the rest of the UK had just spent a year in varying levels of lockdown, Sienna had already been in isolation for half of her life. At just eighteen months old, she was diagnosed with an abscess, but after her mum, Mel, insisted on having a full MRI, it was identified as a tumour. The condition is known as Neuroblastoma, and the tumour was 15cm by 14cm, about the size of a large grapefruit.

Mel described hearing that diagnosis as *"horrendously traumatic"*, not least because Sienna's case was classed as high risk due to her age, the size of the tumour, and the fact that it had already spread to another area. *"All that went through my mind was death,"* she recalled. *"The medics described the worst-case scenario and dispatched us in an ambulance to Great Ormond Street Hospital for emergency chemo. The treatment in the ambulance was outstanding, but I still have flashbacks about that journey now, nearly five years on."*

After five days in Great Ormond Street Hospital, Sienna was discharged to the John Radcliffe Hospital, Oxford, to continue her treatment. But the chemo made no impact on the tumour. Mel says, *"Next they tried an eight-week course of high-intensity chemo, and explained to us she was likely to become very poorly from the side effects. This included measuring her waist before beginning the treatment so they could check whether it was causing her liver to expand. But literally, nothing happened. There were no side effects to the extent expected and no change to the tumour".*

A trial operated through Southampton University was arranged at another London Hospital. This would be a ten-day treatment with an additional fifteen days in absolute isolation because of the radiation levels involved. It would mean anything Sienna had contact with had to be incinerated afterwards. Mel wrote to the makers of Sienna's most-prized possession, "rabbit", explaining the situation and asking for doubles. *"They sent loads, and we spent ages trying to make them look suitably matted to pass as the original rabbit,"* recalls Mel.

As the family prepared to face this frightening ordeal, the situation took another turn. The specialists reported that the tumour was now very close to Sienna's spine, and the risk of paralysis was too high. So the treatment was cancelled, and Mel had to find space for over a dozen duplicate rabbits in their home.

In November 2019, Sienna began a trial at the Royal Marsden Hospital with a new drug. She had to attend the Royal Marsden for treatment three days a week for the first year. Eventually, they were able to administer the drug from home, which reduced the constant travel burden. Thankfully the scans showed positive signs from the drug, with the tumour shrinking by 15% by May 2020. In the meantime, Sienna also had emergency surgery on her spine (which carried a 90% risk of paralysis). Due to the amazing skill of the doctors, she was walking again by Christmas, having spent three months unable to do so.

Despite the trauma and ongoing repercussions of her treatment, Sienna and her twin sister Arianna were eventually able to go to school as the lockdown period eased. Before that, with their two older brothers

Archie and Alfie off school and Mel's partner working long hours as a frontline worker, it was a hectic time at home.

Since the first diagnosis in 2017, it has just seemed like one thing after another for Mel and the family, but they have become a stronger, more resilient, and closer unit as a result. Mel even said she found lockdown "a doddle" compared to the previous years of uncertainty and worry. Once the treatment had started and Sienna's condition became more stable, with the tumour shrinking and her pain controlled by morphine, the family could hold on to hope for the first time in four years.

For me, this story is both moving and inspiring. It reminds me to stop, step back and take hold of some perspective. Most of the time, we live such insular lives that our moods are affected by circumstances within and beyond our control, and our outlook is determined by emotions as fragile as hope. My encouragement to anyone reading this book is to consider Sienna's situation and, like Mel and the rest of her family, be grateful for the opportunity to hope. You simply do not know what tomorrow will bring. But you can add to today – fill your party balloon a little more – by taking hold of hope. Hope costs nothing to produce, just a little time out and perspective.

CHAPTER FIFTEEN

SO THIS IS WHAT FEAR LOOKS LIKE

It's funny how your body gets used to a strenuous routine and starts to rely on the thrill it delivers. This was very evident on the morning after my day off when I jumped out of bed at 5 am and could not wait to get going. It was day sixteen, and I felt like my body was craving the adrenaline rush of pushing against the storm. Scotland was waiting outside, ready to deliver the appropriate conditions. But as it happens, Scotland was the only one that was ready.

Incommunicado and John finds fame

Having arrived only two days before, had the first day cut short by my unscheduled 'forty winks', and then waltzed straight into a rest day, Mike had not yet got into the flow. So, although I now had the companionship I craved, I started the day (which was always going to be a big one) alone. Yet, although I was leaving Mike and Tony in their beds, I felt full of vigour, enthusiasm, and a new rush of excitement when setting out on my solitary start. I was to be incommunicado and all alone for the longest day. I remember thinking then how I had experienced a similar feeling of joy on day twelve. Remember the fell run after sharing my tumultuous Cuil Bay crossing where I met a family of seals? Boggy, nerve-wracking and exhilarating in equal measures. I can easily say that was one of the best adventures of the challenge.

In my opinion, anything that can be described as challenging is usually utterly worthwhile. Such experiences often include surreal moments - like those with the seals and the one I was experiencing right there, on day sixteen, in the middle of nowhere.

What is 'normal' anyway?

I'm sure you have realised this far into the book that I could never be described as 'ordinary'. Anyone who knows me will back that up, and I will readily make that claim. I don't understand why it is. I've checked, and as far as I'm aware, there is no medical condition or psychological profile for the way I embrace what others may see as crazy (or, as some have told me on occasion, irresponsible). The fact is, I don't feel fear, pain, apprehension – even hunger – like 'normal' people do.

This is both an advantage and a disadvantage in life. An advantage because I will go into (almost) all situations without any doubt that I can succeed. A disadvantage because I will go into (almost) all situations without any doubt that I can succeed. It's a double-edged sword!

I fully accept not many will be willing to take on the physical challenges I set for myself. I consider myself exceptionally fortunate that I get to fulfil my inner desire to succeed and exceed in all I do. But believe me, it is just that: a desire. Often, I don't achieve either of those, no matter the effort I put in. I'm trying to explain (and possibly not that succinctly) that I have no fear of putting myself out there and giving anything a go.

It means that provided I use these... personality traits?... quirks?... to the benefit of others, either financially or in a motivational capacity, where people can feel inspired by or learn from my exploits, that can only be a good thing, right? It's what I tell Penny, at least.

The lonely church, the green Land Rover and the missing mobile

Today's plan was to cover a total of 220km, making it the longest day (in terms of distance) of the entire endeavour, so there was no time to lose. Even before I set off, the storm had set in. The rain was falling hard, and it offered no promise of letting up that morning. I was heading west from Durness, along a multitude of coastline climbs and breathtaking descents, determined to get as far ahead of the support team as possible. For the first hour and a half, I didn't see another living soul; then, a local farmer came into view in his green Landrover. He nodded as he passed, in acknowledgement that it was also his first greeting of the day. Or maybe it was his reaction to the surprise (shock?) of seeing a mad cyclist out in that weather, all alone...and at that time of the morning.

Shortly afterwards, I arrived at Eriboll and the tiniest, quaintest little church you've ever seen. Known as 'the rainbow over Eriboll', I thought the lonely situation of this 200-year-old building was really quite profound. It's certainly one of those snapshot visual memories that will stay with me forever.

Laughter is therapy

But there was no time to dwell too long on that thought, and as I pressed on up Sutherland Moor and to the day's highest point, the wind and rain just kept on pounding. It was so wet, and there was so little cover that in the end, I just laughed. I'm not talking about the sort of internal smile you award yourself when the situation is just too much for words. No, this was a full-blown belly laugh. If the Landrover driver had seen me right then, he would have *definitely* thought I was mad!

At that point, my desire to get a good start on the support team turned into wondering why they hadn't yet caught up. So I decided to call them. But, in keeping with the way the day was panning out, I, of course, couldn't find my mobile.

What else could I do?

The missing phone was my third and final. It was the backup for the backup, therefore pretty important. I knew I had it when I was getting ready to leave that morning (checking the essentials had become a habit), so it had to be lost: either en route or outside the campervan itself. Unbelievably, I could see a phone box up there in the middle of that remote Scottish moor. Aha! I would phone Mike and Tony to see if they could check. But their numbers were in the missing phone, so that wasn't going to happen.

The only number I knew 'by heart' was Penny's. You can imagine what she thought when my voice was at the end of the 'unknown number' calling her early that morning. As ever, she reacted brilliantly and soon got the whole situation sorted out, tracking down numbers, making a few calls and saving the day.

Leaving that problem in the safest hands of all (as I said before, even a crazy, one-man-against-the-world struggle needs great external support along the way), I set off into the raging wetness again, forging my way ever closer to the east coast.

In case you're wondering about that lost phone...Mike found it balanced on the end of the cycle rack at the back of the motorhome and was able to pass it back when they caught up with me 80km down the road. Third time lucky: I considered myself a very fortunate boy.

A familiar friend and he's finally found some fame

Mike and Tony finally caught up with me about 80km into the morning. After breakfast, Mike joined me on the bike again as we made our way towards John o'Groats and corner number three of the journey. When we arrived, I have to admit I was a little bit impressed with the place. I'd been there ten years earlier when I was at the start of another adventure (cycling from there to Lands End), and I couldn't believe the changes.

On that occasion, it had been me, a hut and a local guy walking his dog. Now it had become a remote mini-metropolis of tourists and merchants selling their wares in a dazzling array of shops. Mr o'Groats has clearly become quite the celebrity entrepreneur.

As I said, this was the longest single day of the twenty-eight, and although (in our minds) we had started the journey home by reaching that famous landmark, there was still more to do that day. After a kayak across a bay, a short swim, and then a lovely sandy beach run (the weather had turned kinder by then, too), we were back on the bikes for a 50km final leg to Helmsdale.

Twists, turns, tornadoes and close encounters

Helmsdale might sound like the setting for a glorious final battle, somewhere deep inside Tolkien's Middle Earth, but for me, it marked a mighty victory in a long line of battles I had faced in rural Scotland. As we awoke in the carpark of another Brit Stop pub, the Bannockburn Inn (also a little Hobbitish sounding, don't you think?) on day seventeen, it was with an enormous sense of achievement at completing the previous mammoth day.

It seems an obvious observation, but starting on a high can go one of two ways (even better or downhill), and in most cases, that is a choice you make, not a hand that is dealt. As it turned out, this day would be one of the most memorable adventures of all: for a whole host of reasons. It was almost as if it had been taken from the pages of an epic fantasy novel.

The day started early, with the same steady cycle ride as each day of the previous two weeks. This one was a mere 46km before tucking into a tasty bacon butty (or two) for breakfast at Dornoch Golf Course.

Look, Mike! Look at the seals!

After breakfast, Mike joined me for a gentle run along the beach towards what would turn out to be both a challenging and entertaining swim. As we entered the water to cross the Dornoch Firth, we hadn't spotted the abundance of more naturally equipped residents watching our every move. Being his first swim since he'd joined me, Mike was a little wary of even attempting the 2km stretch of open water. The tide was coming in, which was good from a safety point of view but bad from a distance perspective. So we started swimming, and before very long we had company...

I know I had seen them before when we kayaked across Cuil Bay and again around the Northumberland coastline, but even so, it was still a real thrill to see so many seals in such close proximity as they bobbed between us, eager to learn more about these strange 'fish' in their midst. A few even jumped clear out of the water, creating enormous waves and splashes, and I wasn't sure if this was a warning or them simply showing off. I was just excited to be there and take in such a first-hand spectacle. When I turned to share my expressions of joy with Mike, he was simply focused on the far shore, talking with a fair degree of urgency about his desire to see his family just one more time... and being anywhere but here. Apologies, Mike, it's firmly lodged in my memory bank as one of the funniest moments of the trip!

Needless to say, we arrived safely, and Mike quickly regained his sense of humour alongside his keenness to get further along the beach.

Ready, aim, fire!

As we ran along the beach on the other side, more curiosities kept emerging from the sand. These features were neither animal nor mineral but seemed to be relics of a war-torn, long-abandoned past. After we had identified one such structure as a small tank and the next looked suspiciously like an unexploded shell (of the bomb variety), it soon became clear that we had wandered onto a military firing range.

When we finally managed to get reception on the phone to check with Tony, he informed us that it was a Tornado Strike Beach, and there were red flags out indicating that it probably wasn't a good place to be at that time. That's what happens when you enter an area through an unofficial channel rather than the entrance *ordinary* people use! Nobody had thought to put unexploded bomb warning signs on the beach facing the open sea.

After the excitement of the bombed-up beach, we cycled another 25km and from there had a lovely long and leisurely kayak from Balnapaling down to Fort George – we even stopped for a floating lunch on the way.

Storming the fort

Arriving at our destination, I had, for some reason, assumed the imposing-looking fortress looming above us was no longer used, so we just wandered in. Once again, we were approaching the structure from an unusual entry point, not the standard tourist or residents' entrance, and it was no wonder we drew a few curious looks.

Bizarrely, not one of the uniformed soldiers questioned why two wetsuit-clad, kayak-carrying nomads were wandering through the home of Scotland's famous Black Watch Battalion. We could have been anyone. Maybe they had been following my regular blog posts...

That afternoon Mike left me at Fort George and caught a plane back to London; while I got back on my bike for a lonesome 86km ride to my next overnight stop at Findochty. It had been a truly great day, full of surprises, twists, turns and close encounters: but it ended with a tinge of sadness at seeing Mike's departure.

 DAY 16

John o'Groats

Thurso

DAY 17

On to Fort George

Tornado Strike Beach

CHAPTER SIXTEEN

TWO DAYS OF TRUE DIVERSITY

The lonely last leg of yesterday's adventure was soon cheered up by the arrival of another friend from home, Tim Mayes. Tim had met me at Findochty when I arrived, and he had volunteered to lend a hand on this (day eighteen) and the next five days. In truth, his arrival was a huge benefit to me and massively reduced my planning burden in the days to come.

There is a great lesson here for any small business owner who gets so caught up in the job that they are doing and their own destination that they forget how to rely on other people. It can often be underestimated how essential it is to build the right team around you. And however cliched it might sound, every business owner or manager should surround themselves with people better than them. Don't they say, 'you're only as good as your team'? From the moment Tim arrived, it was clear that he wanted to get involved and help. He was a great organiser, a willing worker and full of innovation. I needed Tim.

The day started with a long 95km cycle to Peterhead. As he had only arrived the night before, I did this without Tim, but I did have a prevailing wind for company the entire distance, so it was a truly wonderful treat.

Arriving in the land of the giants!

I had no idea what went on in Peterhead until that trip. I suppose I'd not had any reason to find out other than to look up its coordinates on a map during the planning stages. So I was surprised to discover it is a veritable hive of marine activity, with two gigantic breakwaters enclosing an enormous bay. The ships that loomed way above me were equally spectacular in size as they awaited the call to sail out to a distant North Sea oil rig or two. I felt a bit like Gulliver in Brobdingnag as I launched my tiny kayak into the bay and waited my turn to exit the land of the giants.

The Harbour Master had happily given me the OK to depart, showing great interest in our venture as he watched us prepare to launch from his control tower high above the bay. So I left my newly acquired oversized friends behind and set off into open waters and equally large waves, towering several meters tall. It wasn't violent conditions by any means, but Tim, watching from the harbour wall, said later that it had been fascinating but a little unnerving to watch me bob in and out of view as I paddled by.

I arrived in Boddam and set off on my second cycle of the day, heading down past Aberdeen towards Dunnottar Castle. I went from Gulliver's Travels to a magical and majestic medieval castle that William Wallace had once captured; Dunnottar was a truly magnificent backdrop from which to set off on the final leg of that day's journey.

In a land of aliens

Tim jumped on his bike and joined me for this last off-road ride along a coastal path. Having cycled on solitary tracks, all alone, for so long, it was strange to see a busy menagerie of tourists stretched all along the path. In fact, it was almost like they were the spectacle rather than me for a change. I felt quite out of place – almost like I didn't really belong to the human race anymore.

Although Tim only joined me on the bike for the coastal path, I felt the impact of him being involved the whole day long. It was just good to know I was in the company of someone as committed as me to making the transitions, routes and destinations add up. As I mentioned before, in business, you really cannot grow, move forward or make the changes you need to on your own. You must have good people all around you, and for me, Tim ticked that box completely.

We finished that day at the Harbour Bar pub, in Inverbervie, with a hearty meal, a few well-earned beers and a good night's sleep parked in the carpark.

Movie magic, monumental crossings and a sprint finish

Maybe it was because I'd had such a good night's sleep the night before, but for whatever reason, I started the day cycling in the wrong direction on day nineteen. Possibly a case of over-confidence, or maybe I was subconsciously getting the inevitable mistake out of the way as early as possible in what would turn out to be an otherwise perfect day.

Quickly getting myself back on track, I headed south en route to Tentsmuir Forest, a distance of just under 90km. Despite the minor false start, all the planning I'd been doing late into the evenings and nights was really paying off now. A smooth ride down the coast, then round to Dundee, brought me to the Tay Road Bridge and then straight through to Tentsmuir. The support vehicle was waiting for me, and Tim was even able to cycle up to meet me.

I was joined there by Chris Broome, an ultra-marathon runner and friend of Steven Pike (from my main sponsor, The Marble and Granite Centre). Chris knew the area well, and it was nice to have a guide through the forest, navigating me through the dunes and safely delivering me to the water's edge. From there, I swam the kilometre across the mouth of the River Eden and onto the beach at the world-famous St Andrews Golf Course.

Now you will have to excuse me a little indulgence at this point because I could not resist reenacting the immortal scene from the beginning of the 80s classic movie 'Chariots of Fire', which was filmed here. I didn't go as far as to don the 1920s white shirt and shorts: but it was quite easy to imagine myself surrounded by other aspiring athletes while the famous, mighty anthem by Vangelis slowly built up in the background before rising to a tumultuous crescendo. It was one of those special moments which became a firmly locked memory in my heart and head. (If I am lucky enough to have grandchildren one day, they will either love me or loathe me for the many tales I have accumulated in my head, ready to share in my dotage!)

Aside from the associations with a classic film, the beach was fabulous in its own right, and it was an enjoyable 6km run. From St Andrews, it was back on the bike, and another 50km ride took me round to Queensferry and the Forth Bridge crossing.

Unexpectedly perfect at the Firth of Forth

This was one of the few places where a lack of information had hindered meticulous planning. I simply had not been able to work out a good place to park and launch the kayak. So we literally just turned up hoping there would be somewhere suitable. And, as is often the case when you apply that sort of positivity, we happened upon a perfect spot.

Initially, it looked a little dicey as wind and rain were causing choppy waves. But I was three weeks into my adventure and pretty much ready for anything by now. As far as I was concerned, there had already been too many occasions where the plan had been compromised by caution. And I was so glad that I chose to venture out this time: it was amazing and probably one of the best kayaks so far.

After the first choppy section, I was suddenly paddling with the tide and, with the wind behind me, I was flying. It was almost like being on a hydrofoil, and I barely had time to inspect the work of the perennial painters whose job it is to keep the bridge looking spick and span. The waters then softened to the most idyllic and peaceful image you can imagine as I paddled towards the landing point on Cramond Beach. And the picture I took from there contains one of my favourite memories of the entire trip. In fact, I think the way I incessantly eulogised over the feeling was what encouraged Tim to join me on the next kayaking leg.

A quick taste of city life

Tim also joined me on the bike for the last stretch, which took us through the centre of Edinburgh and East to Aberlady. It was the first time since Liverpool I'd been anywhere near a city centre, and we were both keen to get back out onto the open road. So, with Scotland's capital behind us and a forgiving tailing wind, we set ourselves a self-imposed speed target and went all out to achieve it. An average of 30km per hour saw us arrive at the caravan park for a well-earned rest at the end of another fantastic day.

A new perspective

I described the events of day twenty back in chapter ten and how that simple selfie as I crossed the Scotland-England border over that quirky little chain bridge at Horncliff has become one of my favourites. So I won't repeat or add to the story here. But I would like to remind you of the lesson it taught me about change and why I wrote this book.

You have read about the children and families supported by organisations like Pepper and will be aware that these represent just a handful of thousands of similar stories in the UK. From my exploits, emotions, and life lessons to this point in the journey, I have tried to express what it was like to be there as best I could. Whatever your situation in life, whatever difficulties you face today or your expectations of tomorrow, I believe you can take hold of the day and do something more than sitting and waiting for circumstances to dictate your life to you.

 DAY 18

Cramond Beach

Peterhead

Dunnotar Castle

Stonehaven

CHAPTER SEVENTEEN

DREAMING, PLANNING AND PROCESSING: THE TRUE SPICE OF LIFE

Waking up in England for the first time in over a week felt like a true homecoming, and as I set off on the final quarter of my adventure, I was acutely aware that I was nearing the end. In one sense, such milestone moments drive you to keep going and finish the course, but there was also a tinge of sadness attached to the realisation. Of course, I wanted to get to the end and be able to look back on the accomplishment with a sense of achievement (and a little bit of pride), but I also knew I would miss the daily challenges. For so long, the pain, the excitement, the victories and the extraordinary views set before me each new day had been my companions, and I knew it wouldn't be the same without them.

As if to remind me of the value of the moment; and that I should not linger on the past or the future for too long, Newbiggin-by-the-Sea treated me to a beautiful sunrise as I set off on my first cycle of the day. These were undoubtedly busier roads than I had enjoyed during most of my time in Scotland, and the 'head down' approach had to be reeled in a little. So it was lovely to arrive at the sandy beach of Whitley Bay and get back into the water for a 2km swim. Then, at Tynemouth, it was time to jump in the kayak and make my way around the head of the river and down towards South Shields.

Going around in circles and becoming the fisherman's friend

Reaching day twenty-one meant I had come full circle. Not in my challenge travels, but at the point where I started in the book: the morning

I met fellow kayakers, but they were there because that's how they earn their living. I hope you will realise this on reading the next paragraph because it tells me you have been paying attention and have stayed with me this far! So, I may owe you an apology for repeating myself, although I feel it does bear repeating. Let's call it a bonus 'musing'. However, if the following chapter is news to you because you've skimmed through the book, well...enjoy!

As I ventured into the sea, I was delighted to meet fellow kayakers out on the flat, calm sunny waves. Whereas I was a journeyman traveller just passing by, these guys were professionals, up early and already working. As you'll know from the beginning of the book, I left my new Geordie fisherman friends behind with mutual good wishes shared and a feeling of kinship that I still recall every time I see kippers on a menu! When I think of those fishermen, I consider how we are all fortunate to have choices. Just as many of you reading this book may have chosen to work in an office environment, those fishermen choose to work on the open water. Because most of us are fortunate to have choices, *we* can decide what our life is and what it will become. However, some don't. They are not so blessed and must deal with the hand they have been dealt, like the children supported by The Pepper Foundation.

All I can say is, if you have a choice, don't waste it. Use it. Go for it. Because often, the simple act of 'just going for it' will create the positivity needed to see your goals through, just like my 28 Day Challenge was at first an idea... a vision.

Be a visionary

Today, vision boards are popular amongst entrepreneurs and business owners. I say today, but in reality, they have been with us since the 60s, probably before. You only have to take a cursory look around the internet to find the teachings of some of the legendary business coaches: Earl Nightingale; Napoleon Hill; Lloyd Conant, Zig Ziglar and Bob Proctor. They told entrepreneurs of that era that you can 'think yourself successful'. Many did, many still do – and I'm sure many will use this technique in the future. This generation is not short of a business guru or two (Mr Bezos!).

But you don't have to be an entrepreneur to get value from a vision board. They can support any goal or dream you have. Just remember, however, that alongside having a vision, you need to plan. My vision of the Bonkers Brash Challenge was the easy part. The planning was crucial to its success. For example, one member of our team jumps full pelt into my head when I think about the planning stage of the challenge. Keith Tucker, the personal trainer who had helped prepare me for the venture

Thank you, Keith. Without your incredible work on my body and my mind, I would genuinely not have made it to the end. Positivity can get you a long way, but only a fool would think it doesn't need to be accompanied by hard work of the physical and mental kind. Keith gave me the confidence I could finish *long* before the finish.

A ghostly finish with no sign of Dracula

Landing the kayak after my Tynemouth to South Shields leg, it was back on the bike for what would be the longest cycle ride of the entire adventure. Day twenty-one involved travelling via Whitburn, then Sunderland, through Seaham, then along the charming Durham Heritage Coastline. I whizzed through Hartlepool at lightning speed and followed the River Tees inland at Middlesbrough towards its famous transporter bridge. The longest of its type in the world, and quite a sight to behold, it really is one of those feats of engineering that needs to be seen to be appreciated. Fans of the TV programme Auf Wiedersehen Pet will remember one memorable series where the bridge was sold to Native Americans, dismantled, transported to Arizona and rebuilt. If you haven't seen that episode, take a look, it's funny!

It's all about the timing...

I arrived on the very day the bridge re-opened. It turns out that, after being awarded £2.6m of lottery funding for a refurb, the bridge had been closed since August 2013 and had just started working (for foot passengers only) on the day I arrived in July 2015. What are the chances?!

It is a funny thing that although I can remember most elements of my journey, over those four weeks, in full colour, with pinpoint clarity, the only thing I remember about that part of the journey was the bridge. Sometimes in life and in business, you go through times when everything is just 'going well'. Nothing of note is occurring, good fortune and timeliness give you their favour, and there are no dramas in sight. My advice would be to enjoy them, lift your head up and take in the view. Do positive things, keep the momentum going and drive yourself forward to your destination while the distractions and obstacles are giving you a break.

We met up with Penny's uncle and aunt at Staithes after our timely bridge crossing, and then it was on the bikes for Tim and me for a spooky ride along the Cinder Trail. Tim's help, humour and encouragement over the previous few days had been priceless, so it was lovely to have his company and enjoy the disused railway route, complete with abandoned platforms, empty buildings and the echo of yesteryear. This beautifully and hauntingly serene route from Whitby (the fictional home of Bram Stoker's Dracula) to Scarborough was the perfect way to finish the day and say goodbye to Tim.

Relaxation, reflection and fighting a different battle

Day twenty-two was a rest day in Scarborough, and it was lovely to have Penny and the children with me for my final day off before the big push for the finish line. Relaxing and full-on resting was the order of the day, especially as predictions of poor weather ahead soon arrived. So I was determined to make the most of the day off. Again, this wasn't because I felt I needed it (I was still raring to go) but because I was increasingly learning that it was essential to let common sense have its place occasionally.

I had a much-needed massage, ate well, enjoyed being with the family, spent some time going through the plan for the next few days and indulged in a personal journey of quiet but deep reflection.

Making the time to stop and think

In many ways, it was forced reflection and rest. My body had gone way past being tired and emerged out of the other side feeling unstoppable. For the first time, I started to understand how endurance athletes who take on even greater challenges manage to keep going. It is, quite literally, all in the mind. My body was running on routine, experience and momentum by this point: my mind was where the new battle was happening. Of course, I still needed to take on the right fuel and maintain my muscle health, but essentially I knew that I could just keep on going – whatever. Our bodies are far more resilient and hardy than we could possibly imagine.

So, while I did need the rest, the mental side of doing so was potentially quite dangerous because thinking can go two ways. Fortunately for me, I was surrounded by my family, and I was also laser-focused on finishing what I had started. My big 'life lesson' here is to have a clear vision yourself and be around others who share and appreciate (or at the very least support) what you are trying to achieve.

Don't let the goal spoil the moment

As I indulged and reflected during my final rest day, there was a battle beginning in my mind. On the one hand, I knew I could finish; in fact, I knew that I *would* finish – that question never really became an issue. But I was starting to think about it a bit too much. I began worrying about the weather, not looking forward to travelling routes I'd done before, missing the romance and adventure of Scotland, frightened of the finish because the daily challenge would then be over… and many other mental wanderings.

Eventually, with Penny, the children and common sense as my companions, I settled into a good night's sleep and readied myself for the days to come.

The perfect morning becomes the storm of attrition…

I awoke early on day twenty-three, excited to be back in the saddle with the promise of a fabulous final week of British coastline ahead. The scenery didn't disappoint, but the weather forecast predicted a less favourable few days, with warnings of a storm closing in. Starting early on the bike, I covered the 35km to Bridlington as fast as possible to get the run, swim, and kayak under my belt before the rain belted down. Bizarrely, the water was like a millpond, inviting me to a relaxing kayak, a pool-like swim along the endless South Sands coastline, followed by a picturesque dune-run and back on the bike before dark clouds closed in.

In an instant, the weather changed its mood. It was predicted and expected, but I was still surprised at just how sudden and ferociously the wind and water flared up. Battling horizontal rain, I recalled how often I had wished for a southerly wind in the last three weeks. Finally, nature had graced me with my wish, and oh, how I hated her for it.

Straight through Hull and out the other side...

This was another of those unforeseen changes to the original plan. It bothered me at the time, but in retrospect, it was unavoidable. Life is like that, isn't it? You can never quite predict what will happen, but the fact that you know where you want to go helps keep the course. On the original route, I planned to kayak across the Humber at the Spurn Head nature reserve, but even as I approached the area, it was clear another schedule adjustment was coming. Had I previously completed every other section, as per the original plan, I would probably have attempted it anyway, but having accepted it couldn't be perfect, common sense prevailed. Spurn Head, therefore, still sits on the 'go back and do another day' list.

Although no reflection on Hull, the Humber Bridge (my enforced alternative crossing), or any of the beautiful and scenic locations along that stretch of England's east coast, that particular day was probably the lowest point in the entire month. The extreme weather made the experience just horrible.

For 60km, from Bridlington to Humber Bridge, then a further 100km to Skegness, it was a matter of peddling head-on into wind and sheer rain. I think I soaked up as much dirty water bouncing off the road as there was hurled down, which robbed me of a sight the travel books say is as worth seeing as any in the catalogue of Great Britain's great places to visit. In fact, shortly afterwards, Hull was named the European City of culture. But there are times when circumstance declines you the joy of the moment; that is just the way life ebbs and flows. My memories of the cycling element of that day are 'hard slog'. But here is the thing. Although that day was horrible in every sense of the word, it delivered one of the biggest lessons I learned. Sometimes in life, you simply have to get through the storm in the knowledge that this too will pass. I heard this same thought echoed by the great Tom Hanks recently. It was on one of my favourite podcasts, Kermode and Mayo's Film Review. He said life is like a big bell curve full of good days and rotten days, but each passes by, and in the end, it all evens out. I love that thought.

Corridors of sun-seeking holidaymakers

As I battled my way south, dozens of sun-seeking holidaymakers had passed in slow procession on their way to Skegness. Finally, I caught up with them and entered their land of static caravans and symmetry. And I have never been so happy to get in line as I was that night: one of the crowd, sleeping soundly, protected against the elements and dreaming of better weather. I have to say that a caravan village is not my idea of a holiday destination, but hundreds of thousands of people flock to such places each year, so maybe I am missing something. Whatever that mysterious something is, all I know is that I was grateful to join their tribe for that one night only.

DAY 21

Staithes

Cinder Trail

CHAPTER EIGHTEEN

EMOTIONS STIRRED AND BOXES TICKED

There are marginal decisions and clear-cut ones in any area of life, family, hobbies, business, even love. Both can be disappointments, but equally, both can be rewarding. In my experience, gaining perspective is paramount to making better decisions and dealing with the fallout of making the wrong ones. The next stage of my journey was awash (pardon the pun) with disappointment. The perspective I found was in the reward of a memorable swim and seeing more friendly faces. Sometimes ticking boxes is the best you can do. Moving on through. Not looking back. But learning so you don't make the same mistakes again.

And remember, an achievement is an achievement, no matter what size it is. A tip from me is: always remember 'why'. If you keep that at the forefront of your decisions and subsequent achievements, you'll gain the perspective you need to stay positive.

The washout at The Wash, a memorable swim and friendly faces

On day twenty-four, I had to adapt our plans for the day in response to the weather… again. I had been looking forward to this part of the journey as much as anything I had done before. Traversing Scotland's highland coasts, kayaking down the Menai Strait, and swimming with seals had all been high points. But alongside not being able to paddle across the Severn, what seemed like an age ago, today's washout at The Wash was a massive disappointment.

I intended to launch the kayak from Skegness and paddle the 20km stretch to Hunstanton, but the wind and rain were still shouting 'no'. It was just too dangerous (especially considering the physical effort the previous day had wrenched out of me), and my plans changed again.

Time would not have allowed for me to cycle around and carry on where I would have landed, so I set off instead from Kings Lynn. Later that morning, as I pedalled around the Norfolk coastline with the clouds continuing to empty every last drop of water from their supply, I consoled myself in the pristine beauty of Sandringham Estate. And after the trauma and trial of the day before, my spirits rose even further as I saw Keith (my trainer) waiting to join me for a few days. As I started sharing my adventures with Keith, my focus returned, remembering I was completing a dream rather than sitting behind my desk looking at a computer screen. That was the last time I felt in the least bit sorry for myself on the journey. And seeing the coast again was a great moment, as that part of Norfolk is truly stunning; rightfully designated an area of outstanding natural beauty.

Swimming regardless, but completion on purpose

Arriving at Cromer, we decided it was the best time to fit in the other three elements of my quadrathlon for the day. Before that, however, one of the trip's weirdest moments of synchronicity occurred. As I got off my bike and lifted it onto the support vehicle, the tyre exploded. I have no idea why it chose that moment over any previous hours when I had been *on* the bike or what it was about taking the weight off that made it pop. But that is what happened, and I was so tired it wasn't until months later that I even pondered why.

But now that I have considered what I call synchronicity or others might call good luck or the universe conspiring in my favour, in other words, 'why' – I have come to this conclusion. The secret to keeping mishaps to a minimum with anything mechanical you rely on is to keep things as simple as possible. I did have some unexpected or unfortunate events to deal with along the way, some resulting from human error and others down to just being in the wrong place at the wrong time, but remarkably few were mechanical. Any problems with the equipment tended to be with the more sophisticated kind, like laptops, phones and GPS. But my trusty bike, kayak, paddle, waterproof bag and running shoes were the most solid companions I could have wished for along the way. Simple is secure.

After a beach run and a few kilometres of kayaking, I took to the sea for my required swim, and the wind decided to join in with the waves. It was like a Hawaiian surf without the searing heat and sunlit horizon. Two-metre swells tossed me like a pancake as I forced my way into the deep to complete a reasonable enough distance to claim the day. It is funny how, on reflection, there is very little chance that on a one-off trip to swim on one of Cromer's four beaches, I would have gone through with it on a day like that. But that is what challenges and commitment to a cause will do: push you further.

When you have a goal and the progress to completing that target is well underway, I believe you are in the very best position to make value judgements. The experience, emotion and lessons accumulated along life's way empower you to decide when it is right to adjust and when to press through with the plan. That swim was tricky for sure, maybe even a little dangerous, but I loved it. And the memory floats among my favourites.

Friends, family and reminders of reason

Getting back on the bikes, Keith and I cycled the rest of the day's journey, enjoying a reprise from rain and wind, before arriving tired but happy in Great Yarmouth. Greeting us there (I had almost forgotten this prearranged rendezvous) were two of the team from The Pepper Foundation: Diane Butler and Nicola White. It was really special to see them both and talk about the charity and the challenge. My cousin Rod had also travelled down in style on his motorbike to say a quick hello and lend his support and best wishes. Penny and the children were still journeying alongside the route and completed the welcome guest list during a relaxing evening. I even got to sleep in a Great Yarmouth hotel bed that night – the ultimate lap of luxury.

Happy memories and silly mistakes

The previous day ended in greetings from friendly faces, and the familiarity continued on day twenty-five. I was travelling along a coastline familiar from childhood from here on, and that in itself adds another dimension to any journey. It builds confidence in your mind. You can focus more on what's around you, soaking in the views without worrying about the directions you need to take. By this point, the question of whether I would complete the task was long behind me and the days ahead were full of expectation and excitement. Getting lost through any lack of attention and focus was very unlikely. Or so I thought.

The Essex coastline is fabulous with a distinct personality and very different from what I had been through during the previous weeks. I know it well as my father came from the Chelmsford area, and when I was young, he had a small yacht in a marina on the Blackwater in Essex. We regularly sailed in the rivers, estuaries, and along the coast. Happy days.

Sometimes, however, that same confidence and familiarity (mixed with mental exhaustion) can breed complacency. If you know Great Yarmouth, you will be aware there is no crossing at the headland of the River Yare shipping lane. Why would there be? I knew that, but it didn't stop me from cycling to the end before having to turn around and come back again. It meant a few kilometres more in the grand scheme of things, but I was annoyed with myself about that mindless mistake.

Keeping secrets

Things were soon back on track, however, and 70km later, I arrived in Aldeburgh, a place I also knew well and had been looking forward to seeing again. The stunning Orford Ness nature reserve and conservation area are just south of the town, and it's also the site of a former top-secret Ministry of Defence testing site (but you didn't hear that from me!). In fact, my father once frequented the area while he was working on nuclear triggers, but, once again, I probably shouldn't say any more about that in print. And as I arrived, my focus was miles from secrets of any sort as I went for my swim and run before preparing for a long kayak along the River Alde into another plus 30km an hour headwind.

My launch was delayed, albeit happily, by meeting Penny and the children, who had arrived with my best friend from university, Claire, and her children. I eventually pulled myself away from the rushed catchup and hellos and entered the water an hour and a half behind schedule. Despite hugging the shoreline to combat the relentless wind, the 8km paddle was seriously hard, and by the time I arrived at my exit point, I was even further behind. But it was fabulous to revisit the Orford Ness landscape, and once again, the view and experience were worth every hard-fought paddle.

Friendly faces make all the difference

Another tremendous supporter was waiting to greet me as I emerged from the water. For many years, Chrissy Heeler worked as my personal assistant and bookkeeper for my business. And if I was learning lessons about managing the highs, the lows and the unexpected in a 28-day endurance adventure, Chrissy is someone I have relied on extensively to do the same in my business life for years. I said this earlier: you cannot put a price on having good people in your life. So to see her there as I finished that kayak was just the encouragement I needed.

Keith joined me again for the next leg of the cycling, and we headed south towards Ipswich and on to Althorne, where we finished the day. I am not an overly emotional person, but I was moved by another support act joining for the last 10km of that day's journey. My father died a few years before I set off on this particular adventure, and he had always been a great advocate of my exploits. He encouraged me to keep pushing for the impossible when other people were suggesting I should tone back my ambitions. So seeing his younger brother, my Uncle Mick, at Maldon and chatting together as he peddled (on his 1980s-style, shopping-basket-clad bike) alongside us was wonderful. We reminisced about my dad and pondered what he might have thought and said about this particular quest.

The contemplation, the remembered stories, and the laughter continued at his home in Althorne as we all relaxed in the hot tub with a beer and a wonderful homemade meal.

 DAY 25

Althorne

Thames Creek

CHAPTER NINETEEN

THE THAMES AND THE AUDI DRIVER

I awoke on day twenty-six, totally relaxed. Almost too much at ease in truth. A lovely peaceful evening, comfortable bed, enormous breakfast, friends, family and excellent hospitality are probably not the best preparation for a day of physical exertion. But by this point, there was no question in my mind that I would arrive back in Bournemouth in a few days, on time and with a massive smile on my face. I was physically exhausted but as mentally and emotionally strong as I had ever been.

A tale of two crossings

Not even the future trials of Mucking Creek (yes, really!) and crossing lanes with road-ragers could perturb me from my feeling of confidence that day. Crossing the Thames was always going to be a challenge and, because anywhere east of Tilbury Port is not the most popular tourist attraction on the river, there are few facilities to help. Road access is limited; pathways are non-existent, and thick mud lines traverse both sides of the water. Eventually, we found our way to the aptly named crossing point with its enormous tidal flow; busy shipping lanes, open water wind and choppiness. It was a bit of a gamble, especially as we didn't even know exactly where we might land on the other side, but it was tremendous fun. Keith bravely joined me on the kayak because he was departing as soon as we arrived south of the Thames, and I was glad of the extra paddling power. The view was fabulous with sights of the old docking stations and cranes, and it felt like a significant landmark to safely navigate London's world-famous river.

After forty-five minutes of looking for a suitable landing location amid the murk, we climbed up the bank, emerging like a pair of swamp monsters from the black lagoon. That forty-five minutes might not sound like a lot of time to lose, but on events like this, it is almost impossible to make up lost time; I suppose in the same way it is impossible to relive days that have already passed. As early as day two, I'd started to realise that planning shorter days and allowing larger margins for error would be a better way to go next time. And perhaps that translates into a life lesson. Give yourself more time to get less done as life is much more rewarding that way.

After waving goodbye to Keith and brushing off the now drying mud, I set off towards the populated areas of the Medway towns of Chatham and Rochester. Behind me were hundreds of miles of Great Britain's green and pleasant shoreline, which had mostly graced me with access to sea views, deserted coastal paths, and relaxing seaside towns. But this section was dominated by premium real estate, concrete jungle, traffic hungry roadways and angry drivers on their route from one type of busyness to another.

I'm not in a hurry to return to Medway

A mixture of tiredness, disorientation and failing technology caused a few wrong turns as I navigated roads and tunnels, trying to escape the metropolis. An Audi driver (sorry, but it always seems to be an Audi driver) decided he would rather see me off my bike than on it but failed in his attempt to end my quest two days short of completion. Eventually, I found my escape route and made a bolt for clearer air. Still further from the coast than I would have preferred, I cycled for faceless miles through Sittingbourne, Faversham, Canterbury and across to Sandwich. On a happier note, I remember enjoying a rare tailwind as I peddled away from the madness.

The sun came out to greet me as I reached the coast once more, and the run and swim across Sandwich Bay were absolutely delightful. I slept well in the support vehicle that night.

Weird sands and seven sisters who took my breath away

On the penultimate day of the challenge, I set off early on the bike, rounding the country's southwest corner (at last). I passed Dover and Folkstone, heading towards the sand-blown wilderness of Dungeness. In the previous months, I had seen wonderful sights, both the familiar, new and occasionally unexpected, but nothing quite compared to this. The Dungeness headland wasn't the most spectacular or beautiful place I had visited by any means, but it was the oddest. Aside from the signs declaring restricted areas and nuclear sites, it was like a foreign, almost alien landscape. The sand-blown wasteland looked to stretch for miles, decorated by an eerie people-less silence. And at one point I came across a solitary semi-permanent dwelling, obviously occupied but seemingly lost in time and space. A few years later, I read an article about how, for decades, the authorities have been trying to evict the mysterious lady who lives there, but she is refusing to leave her childhood home.

Whether it was witnessing the phenomenon that is Dungeness or simple forgetfulness, I don't know, but at that point, I checked the GPS for the first time that morning. On doing so, I realised the data had not downloaded properly overnight (I confess to a moment of panic!). I desperately needed a computer and connection to fix the problem, so the message was sent out across Bonkers Brash's social media channels. Eventually, I ended up meeting Neil at the fabulous Kino Cinema in Rye. He kindly let me update my technology for thirty minutes while he showed me around the building. Again, it was a disruption to the day's schedule, but another reminder of how easy it is to ask strangers for help when you are seemingly alone in the middle of nowhere and just how generously people love to respond when you do.

Back on track, enjoying the sunshine and overjoyed to be at nature's coastline once more, I headed back down to Camber Sands and cycled south towards Beachy Head. Although not as famous as their more glamourous cousins back up at Dover, the Seven Sisters Cliffs are stunning. The view as you approach the start of those chalky white escarpments is breathtaking. But not quite as breathtaking as running across them.

A cliff-top run and a peer under the pier

As I traversed 10km of undulating green cliff edge, I marvelled at its height and sheer drop and the vastness of the seascape. It brought back memories of Scotland. The Seven Sisters nickname refers to the number of peaks and troughs as you jog along the top of that part of the coast, and boy is it tough on the legs. Then, descending towards the Cuckmere River estuary, I once again enjoyed the gaze of puzzled onlookers as my run became a swim without so much as a break in momentum.

On the other side and back on the bike, I made my way down to Brighton, where I would kayak 4km along the beachfront, negotiating my way through the crab lines as I navigated under the famous pier. The weather was warming up at last, and small groups of holidaymakers gathered on the beach, some even daring to swim. There was still a bit of a headwind to fight against, but it was a pleasant paddle, and I was adjusting to being around curious strangers once more.

The final stretch was a short 30km cycle to Worthing, then Littlehampton, the location of my campsite for the last night.

DAY 27

Stonehaven

Brighton Beach

CHAPTER TWENTY

MAKE EVERY DAY AN ADVENTURE OF A LIFETIME

I don't know if I had even thought about how I would feel on that final day. I had prepared the previous twenty-seven days down to the finest meticulous detail. As much as possible, I knew where I would physically run, kayak, swim and cover the vast majority of the kilometres by bike. But how do you prepare for emotions? And that was the thing; I really didn't have any. All I felt was the pressure of logistics and ensuring I arrived on time so I didn't disappoint the various people who had travelled down to be a part of day twenty-eight.

I had deliberately made the last day one of the shortest, starting with a 60km cycle to Warsash on the River Hamble. Uncle Mick met up with us again, along with Penny and the children, at the Rising Sun, where Penny's father had lived for a time as a young man. My father would often pile my brother, sister, and me into a dingy here and sail us up the river. So it was the perfect sentimentally charged spot to do the final kayak of the journey. Uncle Mick even joined me as we paddled the calm waters in far kinder weather than most previous crossings, and it was lovely to talk about the old days again.

The end in sight...but is it?

Another 40km of delightful, relaxing and sunny cycling took me through the New Forest's rich greenery to Brockenhurst, where another good friend, Andrew Carmody, and a few of his cyclist buddies joined me for the last part of the cycle. We completed the second part of the New Forest together before arriving in Mudeford, where I prepared for my swim across Christchurch Bay. I once again drew odd looks from passers-by who hadn't the faintest idea what I was doing or why, but that was all part of the fun. Andrew and his mates cycled around the bay while I swam across, and, after completing my run along the beach, we set off to cycle the final stretch to Bournemouth.

The final day and I feel…?

This bit is hard to write because I feel as if it should be momentous. I asked Andrew and the rest of the group to cycle ahead and meet me at the end while I took a moment for the final kilometre. I don't know how long I sat there on my bike, all alone, looking out at the far horizon above the English Channel, trying to find the feeling. But it simply wasn't there. And even all these years later, I'm not sure how I was supposed to feel or behave as I crossed the finish line to loving applause, multiple pats on the back, hugs and congratulations on being – quite frankly – bonkers. The only emotion I could seem to generate was one of slight embarrassment at all the attention and at not shedding any tears of joy or accomplishment.

It wasn't that the completion was an anti-climax. It absolutely wasn't. And I was so grateful for the encouragement, love, friendship, generosity and time given by my family, friends, sponsors and supporters. It was more that the powerful feelings, triumphs, moments, insights and life lessons had been won at previous, often unexpected, times along the way. That was it…

The journey had been more important than the destination

Maybe that sounds like a cliché. But it certainly echoes my life experience to date too.

Each day is precious, and every moment with the potential to deliver unknown adventures is the most valuable of all. I'm sure that is a sentiment held by many now because we are living through the tail end of a pandemic. At the start, when COVID-19 first took hold of our world, turning it upside down and changing all our lives (for many, in truly devastating ways), we heard the word 'unprecedented' …a lot.

It was used in almost every news bulletin and article relating to COVID-19. The dictionary definition of unprecedented is: *never known or done before*. I challenge you to take that word and use it positively. Do something different as often as you can. Venture into the unknown. Seek a life that takes you to your limits and back again. Use due diligence, of course. Risk management is crucial, so don't be reckless, but equally, don't let risk stop you from living life to the full.

I may be bonkers, but for me, that is the only way to live.

 DAY 28

Warsash

Warsash

Me and my Mum

EPILOGUE

WHAT NEXT?

I am writing the final chapter of this book, indeed this epilogue, in April 2022, over six and half years after my epic adventure, and a lot has happened in that time. It would be fair to say the world is a very different place. In a few years, I will be at another milestone in my life, turning fifty, and I can hardly believe it. Wow, the years sure do go quickly.

As I have described and encouraged in the pages you have just read, I believe life is for living, every day should be cherished, and each new dawn signifies the chance to seek excitement and create memory fuel for your life balloon. I have completed many smaller challenges in the last six years and always try to live as much of my life as possible outside of my comfort zone, but my ten yearly challenge is always the 'big one'.

I never underestimate or underappreciate the help and support I am given by family (especially my wife Penny) and friends because I realise how valuable their time is. I know (from decades of positive feedback) that those who get involved in a Bonkers Challenge get a lot out of the experience too, and if it helps them get outside their comfort zone, then maybe I feel a little less indebted to them. I appreciate your time buying and reading this book, and I sincerely hope it inspires you to do something a little more exciting or uncomfortable than you would usually dare to do.

My next big adventure is planned to coincide with that 'big number' birthday I mentioned earlier (don't worry, Penny already knows, she is not reading it here first). In 2025, I aim to complete The Tour Divide, a 2,700-mile self-supported mountain bike race from Banff, in Canada, to the US-Mexico border. In addition to the miles, there are many hills. The total ascent is the equivalent of sea level to the top of Everest, seven times over – beginning with snowy mountain passes and ending in arid desert tracks. Many other aspects of the trip make it a little daunting and quite unlike circumnavigating our green and pleasant lands. For example, one of the few required pieces of equipment I didn't take on my last adventure was anti-bear spray. But what an experience it will be, and I cannot wait to get started.

I'm already thinking about all the planning involved and how three years is not really all that far away. At the moment, all I know is that I will be travelling north to south, following the great Continental Divide, and I also know I will need lots of support from friends and family. I'm not sure about the logistics of getting to the start line yet, or back from the finish line; I don't know if I will undertake this quest alone, have adventurer friends join me on the way or how much training I'll need to do. What I *do* know for sure is that I will be on the start line; nothing will stop that from happening. I know I will have another incredible adventure, and at the end of that journey, there will be far more air from outside my comfort zone squeezed into the party balloon so that I may continue to live life to the full.

Let me know if you fancy getting involved (supporting Pepper, sponsoring some kit, or joining me for part of the journey):
r.brash@brashsolutions.co.uk

ABOUT THE AUTHOR

Richard Brash is far from your ordinary computer geek. Yes, from nine to five on weekdays, he runs a successful IT company in Berkhamsted, Hertfordshire, and loves talking tech and gadgets. But most evenings, weekends, holidays and on the odd week or month-long excursion, he will be doing something outdoorsy (usually muddy, always fun, and occasionally a little dangerous). It is not always solo adventures like the one you'll read about in this book; Richard's family love the thrill of an active outdoor life, too... so do the Scouts group he leads.

Alongside his business interests and Scout work, Richard is also an active member of the Climate Reality Project, promoting climate solutions and the green energy revolution at personal and political levels.

After doing several fundraising events for The Pepper Foundation in the past and seeing the impact their work has on the lives of children with life-limiting conditions, Richard always knew they were the perfect partner for this, his greatest challenge to date. But don't think for a minute that he is finished in his quest to discover his limits. Richard is slowly approaching a milestone birthday and plans to tackle something even more extravagant for that one. Watch this space!

"Breaking speed records is like seeing how far one can lean out of a window without falling out, and therefore somewhat risky" **John Cobb** (World Land Speed Record Holder from 1939 to 1964).

Printed in Great Britain
by Amazon